Scott Foresman
Science

See learning in a whole new light

D1501201

PEARSON
Scott Foresman

Editorial Offices: Glenview, Illinois • Parsippany, New Jersey • New York, New York
Sales Offices: Needham, Massachusetts • Duluth, Georgia • Glenview, Illinois •
Coppell, Texas • Sacramento, California • Mesa, Arizona
www.sfsuccessnet.com

Series Authors

Dr. Timothy Cooney
Professor of Earth Science and Science Education
University of Northern Iowa (UNI)
Cedar Falls, Iowa

Dr. Jim Cummins
Professor
Department of Curriculum, Teaching, and Learning
University of Toronto
Toronto, Canada

Dr. James Flood
Distinguished Professor of Literacy and Language
School of Teacher Education
San Diego State University
San Diego, California

Barbara Kay Foots, M.Ed.
Science Education Consultant
Houston, Texas

Dr. M. Jenice Goldston
Associate Professor of Science Education
Department of Elementary Education Programs
University of Alabama
Tuscaloosa, Alabama

Dr. Shirley Gholston Key
Associate Professor of Science Education
Instruction and Curriculum Leadership Department
College of Education
University of Memphis
Memphis, Tennessee

Dr. Diane Lapp
Distinguished Professor of Reading and Language Arts in Teacher Education
San Diego State University
San Diego, California

Sheryl A. Mercier
Classroom Teacher
Dunlap Elementary School
Dunlap, California

Dr. Karen L. Ostlund
Director
UTeach, College of Natural Sciences
The University of Texas at Austin
Austin, Texas

Dr. Nancy Romance
Professor of Science Education & Principal Investigator
NSF/IERI Science IDEAS Project
Charles E. Schmidt College of Science
Florida Atlantic University
Boca Raton, Florida

Dr. William Tate
Chair and Professor of Education and Applied Statistics
Department of Education
Washington University
St. Louis, Missouri

Dr. Kathryn C. Thornton
Professor
School of Engineering and Applied Science
University of Virginia
Charlottesville, Virginia

Dr. Leon Ukens
Professor of Science Education
Department of Physics, Astronomy, and Geosciences
Towson University
Towson, Maryland

Steve Weinberg
Consultant
Connecticut Center for Advanced Technology
East Hartford, Connecticut

ISBN: 0-328-10001-3 (SVE); ISBN: 0-328-15671-X (A); ISBN: 0-328-15677-9 (B); ISBN: 0-328-15683-3 (C); ISBN: 0-328-15689-2 (D)

Consulting Author

Dr. Michael P. Klentschy
Superintendent
El Centro Elementary School District
El Centro, California

Science Content Consultants

Dr. Frederick W. Taylor
Senior Research Scientist
Institute for Geophysics
Jackson School of Geosciences
The University of Texas at Austin
Austin, Texas

Dr. Ruth E. Buskirk
Senior Lecturer
School of Biological Sciences
The University of Texas at Austin
Austin, Texas

Dr. Cliff Frohlich
Senior Research Scientist
Institute for Geophysics
Jackson School of Geosciences
The University of Texas at Austin
Austin, Texas

Brad Armosky
McDonald Observatory
The University of Texas at Austin
Austin, Texas

 Content Consultants

Adena Williams Loston, Ph.D.
Chief Education Officer
Office of the Chief Education Officer

Clifford W. Houston, Ph.D.
Deputy Chief Education Officer for Education Programs
Office of the Chief Education Officer

Frank C. Owens
Senior Policy Advisor
Office of the Chief Education Officer

Deborah Brown Biggs
Manager, Education Flight Projects Office
Space Operations Mission Directorate, Education Lead

Erika G. Vick
NASA Liaison to Pearson Scott Foresman
Education Flight Projects Office

William E. Anderson
Partnership Manager for Education
Aeronautics Research Mission Directorate

Anita Krishnamurthi
Program Planning Specialist
Space Science Education and Outreach Program

Bonnie J. McClain
Chief of Education
Exploration Systems Mission Directorate

Diane Clayton, Ph.D.
Program Scientist
Earth Science Education

Deborah Rivera
Strategic Alliances Manager
Office of Public Affairs
NASA Headquarters

Douglas D. Peterson
Public Affairs Officer, Astronaut Office
Office of Public Affairs
NASA Johnson Space Center

Nicole Cloutier
Public Affairs Officer, Astronaut Office
Office of Public Affairs
NASA Johnson Space Center

Dr. Jennifer J. Wiseman
Hubble Space Telescope Program Scientist
NASA Headquarters

Reviewers

Dr. Maria Aida Alanis
Administrator
Austin ISD
Austin Texas

Melissa Barba
Teacher
Wesley Mathews Elementary
Miami, Florida

Dr. Marcelline Barron
Supervisor/K-12 Math
and Science
Fairfield Public Schools
Fairfield, Connecticut

Jane Bates
Teacher
Hickory Flat Elementary
Canton, Georgia

Denise Bizjack
Teacher
Dr. N. H. Jones Elementary
Ocala, Florida

Latanya D. Bragg
Teacher
Davis Magnet School
Jackson, Mississippi

Richard Burton
Teacher
George Buck Elementary
School 94
Indianapolis, Indiana

Dawn Cabrera
Teacher
E.W.F. Stirrup School
Miami, Florida

Barbara Calabro
Teacher
Compass Rose Foundation
Ft. Myers, Florida

Lucille Calvin
Teacher
Weddington Math &
Science School
Greenville, Mississippi

Patricia Carmichael
Teacher
Teasley Middle School
Canton, Georgia

Martha Cohn
Teacher
An Wang Middle School
Lowell, Massachusetts

Stu Danzinger
Supervisor
Community Consolidated
School District 59
Arlington Heights, Illinois

Esther Draper
Supervisor/Science Specialist
Belair Math Science
Magnet School
Pine Bluff, Arkansas

Sue Esser
Teacher
Loretto Elementary
Jacksonville, Florida

Dr. Richard Fairman
Teacher
Antioch University
Yellow Springs, Ohio

Joan Goldfarb
Teacher
Indialantic Elementary
Indialantic, Florida

Deborah Gomes
Teacher
A J Gomes Elementary
New Bedford, Massachusetts

Sandy Hobart
Teacher
Mims Elementary
Mims, Florida

Tom Hocker
Teacher/Science Coach
Boston Latin Academy
Dorchester, Massachusetts

Shelley Jaques
Science Supervisor
Moore Public Schools
Moore, Oklahoma

Marguerite W. Jones
Teacher
Spearman Elementary
Piedmont, South Carolina

Kelly Kenney
Teacher
Kansas City Missouri
School District
Kansas City, Missouri

Carol Kilbane
Teacher
Riverside Elementary School
Wichita, Kansas

Robert Kolenda
Teacher
Neshaminy School District
Langhorne, Pennsylvania

Karen Lynn Kruse
Teacher
St. Paul the Apostle
Yonkers, New York

Elizabeth Loures
Teacher
Point Fermin
Elementary School
San Pedro, California

Susan MacDougall
Teacher
Brick Community Primary
Learning Center
Brick, New Jersey

Jack Marine
Teacher
Raising Horizons Quest
Charter School
Philadelphia, Pennsylvania

Nicola Micozzi Jr.
Science Coordinator
Plymouth Public Schools
Plymouth, Massachusetts

Paula Monteiro
Teacher
A J Gomes Elementary
New Bedford, Massachusetts

Tracy Newallis
Teacher
Taper Avenue Elementary
San Pedro, California

Dr. Eugene Nicolo
Supervisor, Science K-12
Moorestown School District
Moorestown, New Jersey

Jeffry Pastrak
School District of Philadelphia
Philadelphia, Pennsylvania

Helen Pedigo
Teacher
Mt. Carmel Elementary
Huntsville Alabama

Becky Peltonen
Teacher
Patterson Elementary School
Panama City, Florida

Sherri Pensler
Teacher/ESOL
Claude Pepper Elementary
Miami, Florida

Virginia Rogliano
Teacher
Bridgeview Elementary
South Charleston, West
Virginia

Debbie Sanders
Teacher
Thunderbolt Elementary
Orange Park, Florida

Grethel Santamarina
Teacher
E.W.F. Stirrup School
Miami, Florida

Migdalia Schneider
Teacher/Bilingual
Lindell School
Long Beach, New York

Susan Shelly
Teacher
Bonita Springs Elementary
Bonita Springs, Florida

Peggy Terry
Teacher
Madison Elementary
South Holland, Illinois

Jane M. Thompson
Teacher
Emma Ward Elementary
Lawrenceburg, Kentucky

Martha Todd
Teacher
W. H. Rhodes Elementary
Milton, Florida

Renee Williams
Teacher
Bloomfield Schools
Central Primary
Bloomfield, New Mexico

Myra Wood
Teacher
Madison Street Academy
Ocala, Florida

Marion Zampa
Teacher
Shawnee Mission
School District
Overland Park, Kansas

Science

See learning in a whole new light

How to Read Science xx

Science Process Skills xxii

Using Scientific Methods xxvi

Science Tools xxviii

Safety in Science xxxii

Unit A Life Science

What do living things need?

Chapter 1 • Living and Nonliving

Build Background 2

Lab zone **Directed Inquiry Explore** Which is a living thing? . 4

How to Read Science Alike and Different 5

Chapter Song "Is It Living? I'd Like to Know!" 6

Lesson 1 • What are living things? 7

Lesson 2 • What do plants need? 10

Lesson 3 • What do animals need? 12

Lesson 4 • What are nonliving things? 14

Lab zone **Guided Inquiry Investigate** How do brine shrimp eggs change in salt water? 18

Math in Science Sorting and Counting Living and Nonliving Things 20

Chapter 1 Review and Test Prep 22

Biography Dr. Sonia Ortega 24

Chapter 2 • Habitats

Build Background 26

Directed Inquiry Explore Where do animals live? 28

How to Read Science Picture Clues 29

Chapter Song "Habitats" 30

Lesson 1 • What is a forest habitat? 31

Lesson 2 • What is a wetland habitat? 34

Lesson 3 • What is an ocean habitat? 36

Lesson 4 • What is a desert habitat? 38

Guided Inquiry Explore How do desert leaves hold water? 40

Math in Science Counting Animals 42

Chapter 2 Review and Test Prep 44

NASA Habitats at Kennedy Space Center 46

Career Naturalists 48

Where do plants and animals live?

Unit A Life Science

How do parts help living things?

Chapter 3 • How Plants and Animals Live

Build Background 50

Lab zone **Directed Inquiry Explore** How can fur keep animals warm? 52

How to Read Science Alike and Different . . . 53

Chapter Song "Something Special" 54

Lesson 1 • What helps animals live in their habitats? . . 55

Lesson 2 • How do animals get food? 58

Lesson 3 • What can help protect animals? 62

Lesson 4 • What are some parts of plants? 68

Lesson 5 • What helps protect plants? 72

Lab zone **Guided Inquiry Investigate** Which leaf shape drips faster? 74

Math in Science Classify Animals 76

Chapter 3 Review and Test Prep 78

NASA **Career** Medical Researcher 80

Chapter 4 • Life Cycles

Build Background 82

Lab zone **Directed Inquiry Explore** How do mealworms change as they grow? 84

How to Read Science Put Things in Order . . . 85

Chapter Song "That's a Life Cycle" 86

Lesson 1 • How does a frog grow? 87

Lesson 2 • How does a butterfly grow? 92

Lesson 3 • How do animals grow and change? 94

Lesson 4 • How does a daisy grow?. 98

Lesson 5 • How do trees grow? 100

Lesson 6 • How do plants grow and change? 104

Lab zone **Guided Inquiry Investigate** How do seeds change? 106

Math in Science Comparing Size and Age 108

Chapter 4 Review and Test Prep. 110

Career Doctors 112

How do animals and plants grow and change?

Unit A Life Science

How are living things connected?

Chapter 5 • Food Chains

Build Background 114

Lab zone Directed Inquiry Explore What do animals eat? 116

How to Read Science Draw Conclusions . . 117

Chapter Song "Round and Round and Round" 118

Lesson 1 • How do plants and animals get food?. . . 119

Lesson 2 • How do living things get food
in a rain forest? 122

Lesson 3 • How do living things get food in a marsh?. 126

Lab zone Guided Inquiry Investigate How can you
make a model of a food chain? 130

Math in Science Grouping Animals 132

Chapter 5 Review and Test Prep. 134

Career Entomologists 136

 **Unit A Test Talk** 137

Unit A Wrap-Up 138

Lab zone **Full Inquiry Experiment** How can camouflage
help mice stay hidden from hawks? 140

End with a Poem "The Frog on the Log" 142

Science Fair Projects:
Growing Plants in Soil; What Birds Eat 144

Unit B Earth Science

How are land, water, and air important?

Chapter 6 • Land, Water, and Air

Build Background 146

Lab zone **Directed Inquiry Explore** How can you make a model of land and water? 148

How to Read Science Important Details . . . 149

Chapter Song "Water, Air, and Land" 150

Lesson 1 • What makes up Earth? 151

Lesson 2 • What are rocks and soil? 154

Lesson 3 • What changes land? 158

Lesson 4 • How do living things use natural resources? 160

Lesson 5 • How can you reduce, reuse, and recycle? . 166

Lab zone **Guided Inquiry Investigate** How are these soils different? 168

Math in Science Reading a Picture Graph 170

Chapter 6 Review and Test Prep 172

NASA Satellites Help Scientists Find Fossils 174

Biography Dr. Winifred Goldring 176

WE RECYCLE

Chapter 7 • Weather

Build Background 178

Lab zone **Directed Inquiry Explore** How can you tell
when it is windy? 180

How to Read Science Predict 181

Chapter Song "Can I Go Outside and Play?" 182

Lesson 1 • How can you measure weather? 183

Lesson 2 • How do clouds form? 186

Lesson 3 • What are some kinds of wet weather? . . 188

Lesson 4 • What are the four seasons? 192

Lab zone **Guided Inquiry Investigate** How does
the temperature change each day? 194

Math in Science Using a Bar Graph 196

Chapter 7 Review and Test Prep 198

NASA **Career** Meteorologist 200

Unit B Test Talk 201

Unit B Wrap-Up 202

Lab zone **Full Inquiry Experiment** Does the Sun warm
land or water faster? 204

End with a Poem "Wind" 206

Science Fair Projects:
Comparing Temperature; Erosion 208

What are the four seasons?

Unit C Physical Science

How can objects be described?

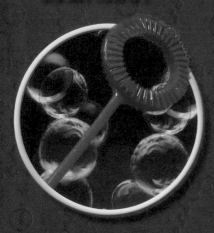

Chapter 8 • Observing Matter

Build Background 210

Lab zone **Directed Inquiry Explore** What is in the bag? . 212

Target Skill **How to Read Science Alike and Different** . . 213

Chapter Song "A 'Matter' of Lemonade" 214

Lesson 1 • What is matter? 215

Lesson 2 • What are solids, liquids, and gases? . . . 218

Lesson 3 • How does matter change? 222

Lesson 4 • How can water change? 226

Lesson 5 • What are other ways matter changes? . . 230

Lab zone **Guided Inquiry Investigate**
Will it float or sink? 232

Math in Science Comparing Height and Weight . . . 234

Chapter 8 Review and Test Prep 236

NASA Matter on the Moon 238

Career Blowing Glass 240

Chapter 9 • Movement and Sound

What makes objects move?

Build Background 242

Directed Inquiry Explore How can you move the car? 244

How to Read Science Cause and Effect . . . 245

Chapter Song "Pull the Sled!" 246

Lesson 1 • What makes things move? 247

Lesson 2 • What is speed? 250

Lesson 3 • How do things move? 252

Lesson 4 • What do magnets do? 256

Lesson 5 • How are sounds made? 260

Lesson 6 • What sounds are around us? 262

Guided Inquiry Investigate
What do you hear? 266

Math in Science Speed 268

Chapter 9 Review and Test Prep 270

Biography Dr. Shamin Rhamin 272

Unit C Physical Science

Where does energy come from?

Chapter 10 • Learning About Energy

Build Background 274

Directed Inquiry Explore Can the Sun's light
heat water? 276

How to Read Science Draw Conclusions . . 277

Chapter Song "Energy" 278

Lesson 1 • What gives off heat?. 279

Lesson 2 • What can energy do? 282

Lesson 3 • What makes light and shadows? 284

Lesson 4 • What uses energy around us? 290

Lesson 5 • How do you get energy?. 294

Guided Inquiry Investigate
How can you make a shadow? 298

Math in Science Reading a Picture Graph 300

Chapter 10 Review and Test Prep 302

Biography Felix Alberto Soto Toro 304

Unit C Test Talk 305

Unit C Wrap-Up 306

Full Inquiry Experiment
How can you make high and low sounds? 308

End with a Poem "Merry-Go-Round" 310

Science Fair Projects:
Energy in an Aquarium; Energy in a Terrarium . . 312

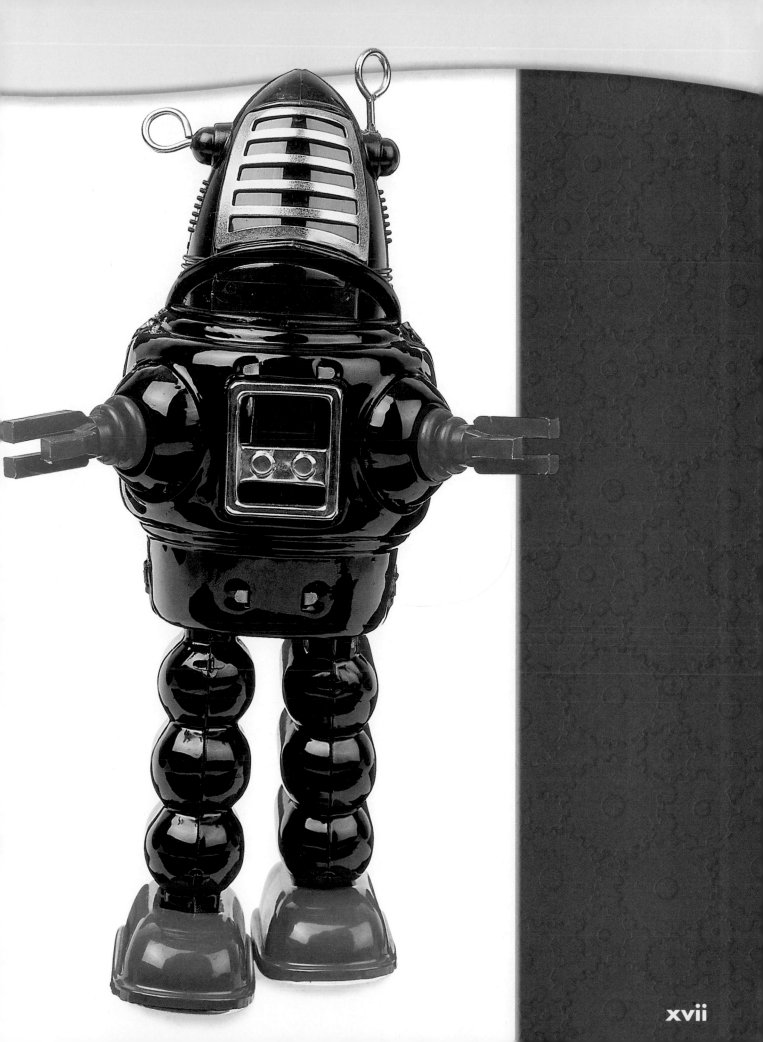

Unit D Space and Technology

What is in the sky?

Chapter 11 • Day and Night Sky

Build Background 314

Directed Inquiry Explore Why does the Sun
look small? 316

How to Read Science Important Details . . . 317

Chapter Song "Look Up High!" 318

Lesson 1 • What is in the day sky? 319

Lesson 2 • What causes day and night? 322

Lesson 3 • What is in the night sky? 324

Guided Inquiry Investigate Why do you
see things in the night sky? 328

Math in Science Reading a Calendar 330

Chapter 11 Review and Test Prep 332

NASA Exploring the Sky 334

NASA Career Astronauts 336

Chapter 12 • Science in Our World

Build Background 338

Lab zone **Directed Inquiry Explore** How can you use tools? 340

How to Read Science Put Things in Order . . 341

Chapter Song "Technology Helps" 342

Lesson 1 • How do farmers use technology to grow food? 343

Lesson 2 • How does food get from the farm to the store? 346

Lesson 3 • What tools can you use to make dinner? . 348

Lesson 4 • How do builders get wood for a house?. . 352

Lesson 5 • What are simple machines? 356

Lesson 6 • What can you use to communicate?. . . . 360

Lab zone **Guided Inquiry Investigate** How can you build a strong bridge? 362

Math in Science Classifying Plant Parts 364

Chapter 12 Review and Test Prep 366

NASA **Biography** Mike Wong 368

Unit D Test Talk 369

Unit D Wrap-Up 370

Lab zone **Full Inquiry Experiment** How can a smaller person lift a bigger person in a seesaw? 372

End with a Poem "Taking Off" 374

Discovery School **Science Fair Projects:** Making Paper Airplanes; Changing a Wheel . . . 376

Metric and Customary Measurement EM1

Glossary EM2

Index EM22

Acknowledgments and Credits EM28

How does technology help people?

How to Read Science

Each chapter in your book has a page like this one. This page shows you how to use a reading skill.

Before reading
First, read the Build Background page. Next, read the How To Read Science page. Then, think about what you already know. Last, make a list of what you already know.

Target Reading Skill
The target reading skill will help you understand what you read.

Real-World Connection
Each page has an example of something you will learn.

Graphic Organizer
A graphic organizer can help you think about what you learn.

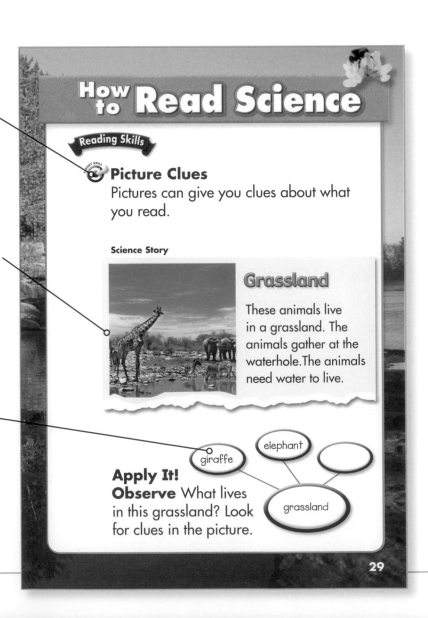

How to Read Science

Reading Skills

Picture Clues
Pictures can give you clues about what you read.

Science Story

Grassland
These animals live in a grassland. The animals gather at the waterhole. The animals need water to live.

Apply It!
Observe What lives in this grassland? Look for clues in the picture.

giraffe · elephant · grassland

29

Map Facts
A swamp is a wetland. Okefenokee Swamp in Georgia has about 70 islands.

crane

dragonfly

bullfrog

✓ **Lesson Checkpoint**
1. What does a duck get in a wetland?
2. 🎯 Use **picture clues** to tell what animals live in a wetland.

35

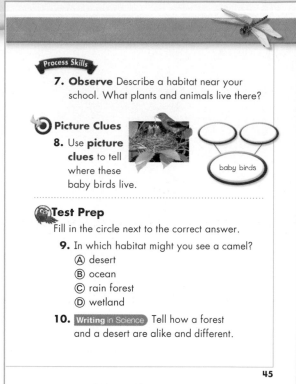

Process Skills
7. **Observe** Describe a habitat near your school. What plants and animals live there?

🎯 **Picture Clues**
8. Use **picture clues** to tell where these baby birds live.

baby birds

🦉 **Test Prep**
Fill in the circle next to the correct answer.
9. In which habitat might you see a camel?
   Ⓐ desert
   Ⓑ ocean
   Ⓒ rain forest
   Ⓓ wetland
10. Writing in Science Tell how a forest and a desert are alike and different.

45

🎯 During reading

Use the checkpoint as you read the lesson. This will help you check how much you understand.

🎯 After reading

Think about what you have learned. Compare what you learned with the list you made before you read the chapter. Answer the questions in the Chapter Review.

Target Reading Skills

These are some target reading skills that appear in this book.

- Cause and Effect
- Alike and Different
- Put Things in Order
- Predict

- Draw Conclusions
- Picture Clues
- Important Details

Science Process Skills

Observe

A scientist who wants to find out about the ocean observes many things. You use your senses to find out about things too.

Classify

Scientists classify living things in the ocean. You classify when you sort or group things by their properties.

Estimate and Measure

Scientists can estimate the size of living things in the ocean. This means they make a careful guess about the size or amount of something. Then they measure it.

Infer

Scientists are always learning about living things in the ocean. Scientists draw a conclusion or make a guess from what they already know.

Under the Water

Scientists use process skills to find out about things. You will use these skills when you do the activities in this book. Suppose scientists want to learn about living things in the ocean. Which process skills might they use?

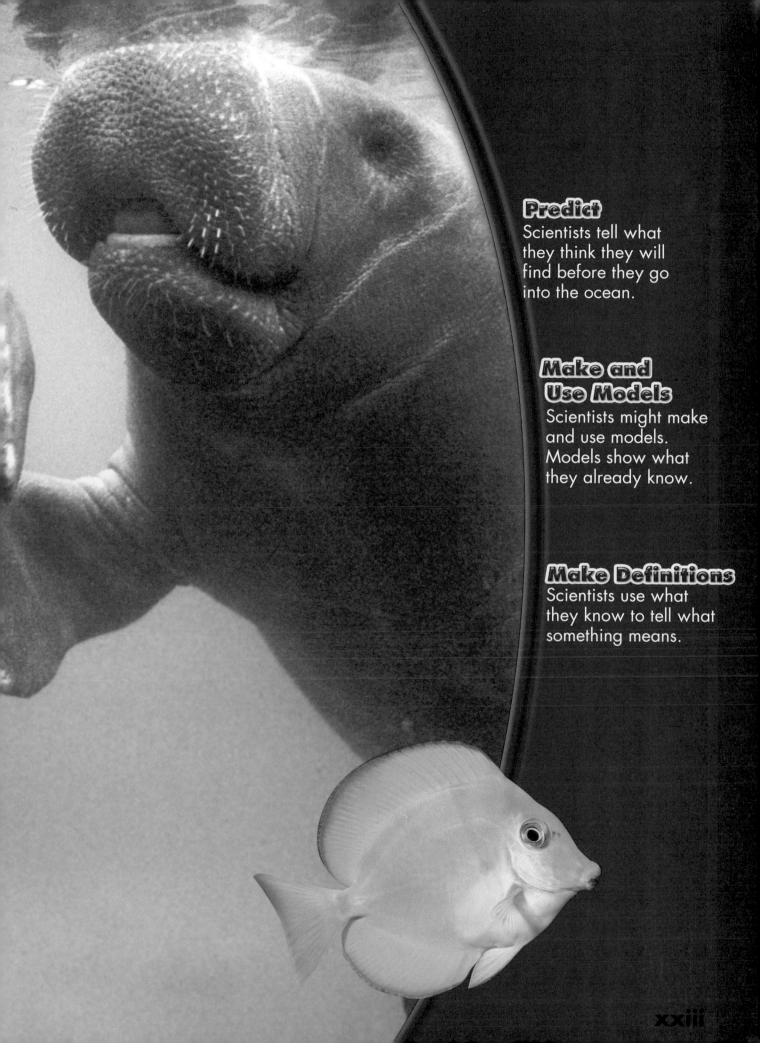

Predict

Scientists tell what they think they will find before they go into the ocean.

Make and Use Models

Scientists might make and use models. Models show what they already know.

Make Definitions

Scientists use what they know to tell what something means.

Science Process Skills

Make Hypotheses

Think of a question you have about living things in the ocean. Make a statement that you can test to answer your question.

Collect Data

Scientists record what they observe and measure. Scientists put this data into charts or graphs.

Interpret Data

Scientists use what they learn to solve problems or answer questions.

Suppose you were a scientist. You might want to learn more about the ocean. What questions might you have? How would you use process skills to help you learn?

Investigate and Experiment
Scientists plan and do an investigation as they study the ocean.

Control Variables
Scientists plan a fair test. Scientists change only one thing in their test. Scientists keep everything else the same.

Communicate
Scientists tell what they learn about living things in the ocean.

Using Scientific Methods

Scientific methods are ways of finding answers. Scientific methods have these steps. Sometimes scientists do the steps in a different order. Scientists do not always do all of the steps.

Ask a question.

Ask a question that you want answered.

Do seeds need water to grow?

Make your hypothesis.

Tell what you think the answer is to your question.

If seeds are watered, then they will grow.

Plan a fair test.

Change only one thing.

Keep everything else the same.

Water one pot with seeds.

no water

water

Do your test.

Test your hypothesis. Do your test more than once. See if your results are the same.

Collect and record your data.

Keep records of what you find out. Use words or drawings to help.

Tell your conclusion.

Observe the results of your test. Decide if your hypothesis is right or wrong. Tell what you decide.

Seeds need water to grow.

no water

water

Go further.

Use what you learn. Think of new questions or better ways to do a test.

Ask a Question

Make Your Hypothesis

Plan a Fair Test

Do Your Test

Collect and Record Your Data

Tell Your Conclusion

Go Further

Science Tools

Scientists use many different kinds of tools.

Measuring cup
You can use a measuring cup to measure volume. Volume is how much space something takes up.

Stopwatch
A stopwatch measures how much time something takes.

Computer
You can learn about science at a special Internet website. Go to www.sfsuccessnet.com.

Ruler
You can use a ruler to measure how long something is. Most scientists use a ruler to measure length in centimeters or millimeters.

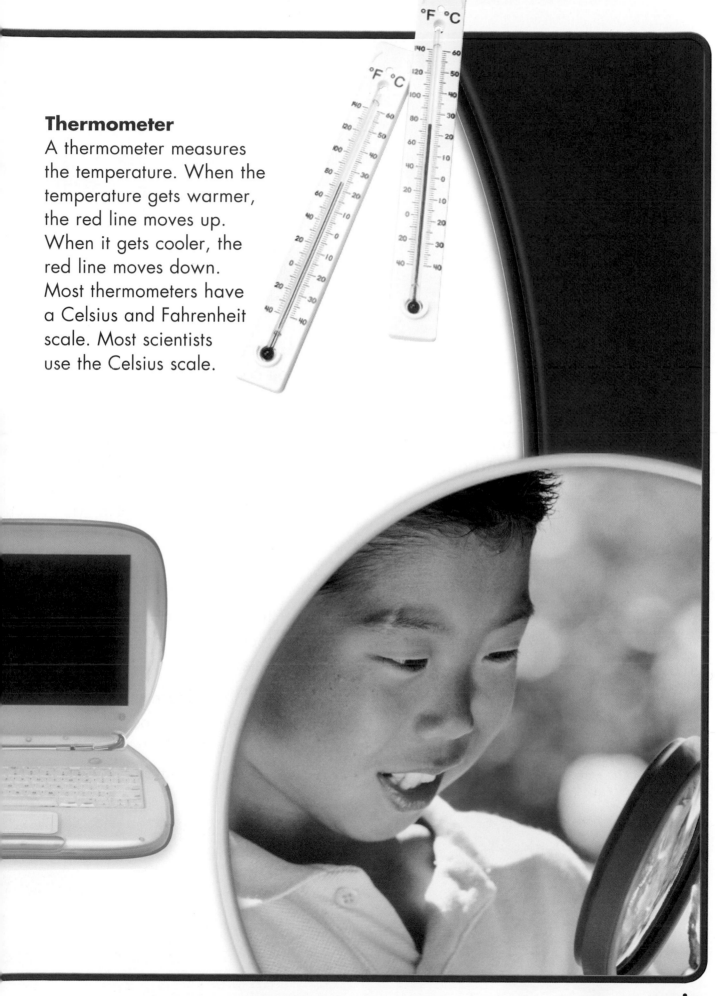

Thermometer

A thermometer measures the temperature. When the temperature gets warmer, the red line moves up. When it gets cooler, the red line moves down. Most thermometers have a Celsius and Fahrenheit scale. Most scientists use the Celsius scale.

Science Tools

Safety goggles
You can use safety goggles to protect your eyes.

Calculator
A calculator can help you do things, such as add and subtract.

Balance
A balance is used to measure the mass of objects. Mass is how much matter an object has. Most scientists measure mass in grams or kilograms.

Meterstick
You can use a meterstick to measure how long something is too. Scientists use a meterstick to measure in meters.

Clock
A clock measures time.

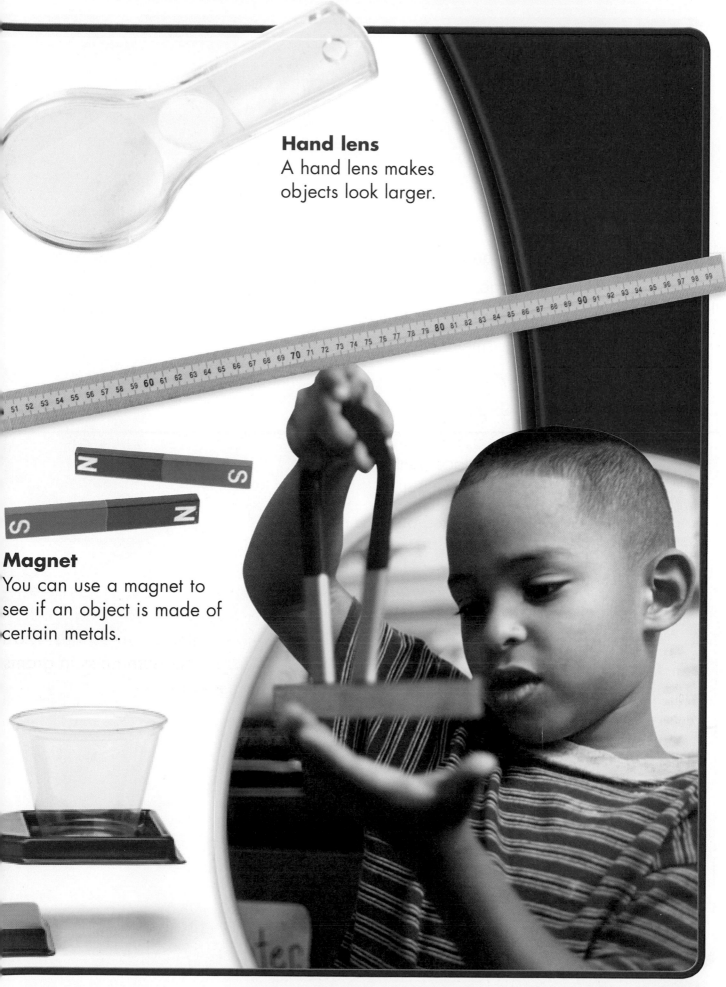

Hand lens
A hand lens makes objects look larger.

Magnet
You can use a magnet to see if an object is made of certain metals.

Safety in Science

You need to be careful when doing science activities. This page includes safety tips to remember:

- Listen to your teacher's instructions.
- Never taste or smell materials unless your teacher tells you to.
- Wear safety goggles when needed.
- Handle scissors and other equipment carefully.
- Keep your work place neat and clean.
- Clean up spills immediately.
- Tell your teacher immediately about accidents or if you see something that looks unsafe.
- Wash your hands well after every activity.

Unit A

Life Science

Chapter 1
Living and Nonliving

You Will Discover

- why living things are alive.
- that nonliving things were never alive.

online
Student Edition
sfsuccessnet.com

What do living things need?

living

shelter

2

Chapter 1 Vocabulary

living page 7

shelter page 12

nonliving page 14

nonliving

Explore Which is a living thing?

Materials

bowl with gravel

bean seeds

cup with water

What to Do

1 Put the bean seeds on the gravel.

2 Cover the gravel with water. Observe for 4 days.

Explain Your Results
Observe what happens. Tell about the changes you see.

How to Read Science

Alike and Different

Alike means how things are the same. Different means how things are not the same.

Science Pictures

Apply It!
Observe the trees. How are the trees alike and different?

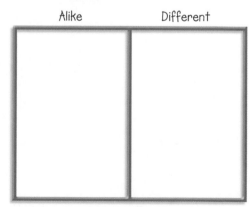

Alike	Different

5

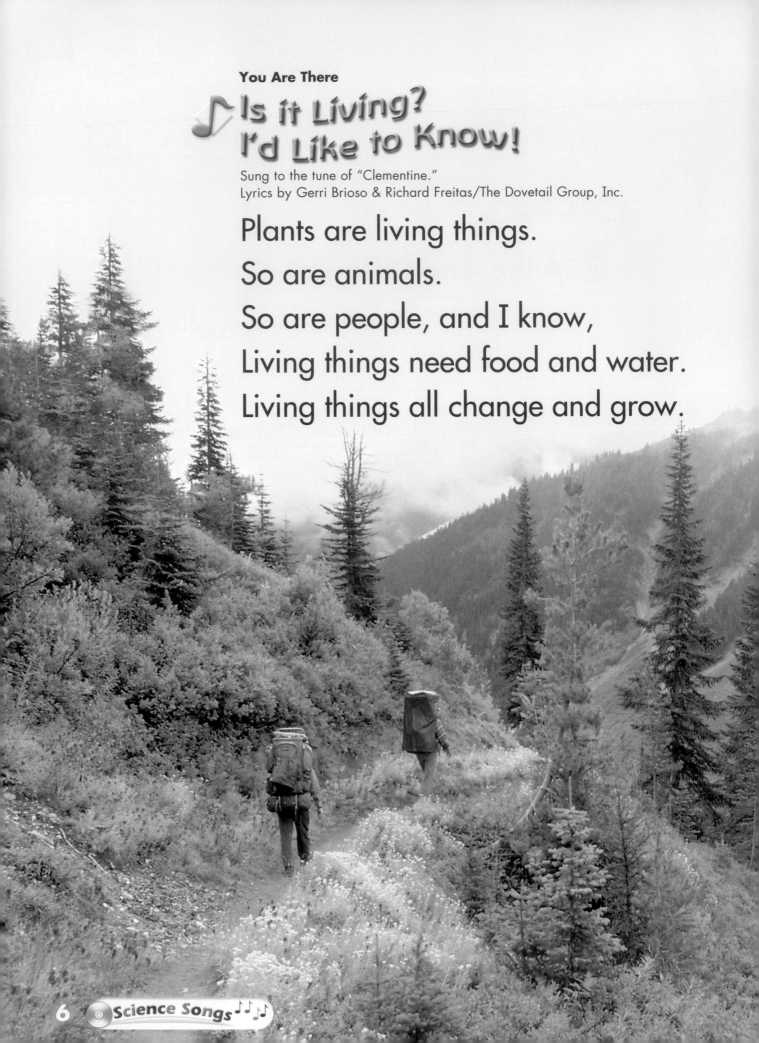

♪ Is it Living? I'd Like to Know!

Sung to the tune of "Clementine."
Lyrics by Gerri Brioso & Richard Freitas/The Dovetail Group, Inc.

Plants are living things.

So are animals.

So are people, and I know,

Living things need food and water.

Living things all change and grow.

Lesson 1
What are living things?

Living things are alive.
Living things can grow.
Living things can change.

Plants are living things.
Animals are living things.
People are living things too.

This butterfly is a living thing.

Plants and Animals

Plants can grow.
Plants can change.

Animals can grow.
Animals can change.

Grown animals can
have young animals.

Many animals can
move on their own.

**This young oak
tree will grow.**

8

How do these animals move?

✓**Lesson Checkpoint**

1. What is a living thing?

2. **Math** in Science What could you use to measure how tall the young oak tree is?

9

What do plants need?

A need is something a living thing must have to live.

Plants need air and water.
Plants need light from the Sun.
Plants need space to live and grow.

Rain can give plants the water they need.

✓ **Lesson Checkpoint**

1. What do plants need to live?

2. **Writing** in Science   Tell how plants can get water.

What do animals need?

Animals have needs too.
Animals need food.
Animals need water.
Animals need air.

Animals need space to live.
Some animals need shelter.
A **shelter** is a safe place.

Munch!
The chipmunk eats flower parts for food.

The birds use a nest for shelter. This nest is made of sticks and grasses.

What does this wolf pup use for shelter?

✓ Lesson Checkpoint

1. What do animals need to live?

2. 🎯 How are the needs of plants and animals **alike and different**?

Lesson 4

What are nonliving things?

Nonliving things were never alive. Nonliving things do not need food and water.

Nonliving things do not grow on their own.
Nonliving things do not change on their own.

1. ✓**Checkpoint** How do you know that a chair is a nonliving thing?

2. **Writing** in Science Draw a picture of a nonliving thing. Write one sentence about your picture.

Look at the classroom. What nonliving things do you see?

Nonliving Things Around You

People make some nonliving things. People make some toys that look like living things. People make some toys that move like living things.

Name some nonliving things in the bathtub.

There are nonliving
things in nature.
Water is a nonliving thing.
Water does not need food.
Water does not grow.

What nonliving things do you see in this picture?

✓ **Lesson Checkpoint**

1. What are some nonliving things made by people?

2.  How are a toy dog and a living dog **alike and different**?

Investigate How do brine shrimp eggs change in salt water?

Materials

spoon with shrimp eggs

hand lens

cup with salt water

What to Do

1 Look at the shrimp eggs with a hand lens. Draw a picture to show how they look.

2 Add the shrimp eggs to the salt water.

Process Skills

You **interpret data** when you use data to answer questions.

3 Observe the eggs for 5 days.

4 **Collect Data** Draw a picture each day to show what happens to the shrimp eggs.

Observing Brine Shrimp				
Day 1	Day 2	Day 3	Day 4	Day 5

Explain Your Results

1. **Interpret Data** What changes did you observe in 5 days?

2. What do brine shrimp eggs need to grow and change?

Go Further

Could shrimp eggs live in water that is not salty? How could you find out?

Sorting and Counting Living and Nonliving Things

e Tools Take It to the Net
sfsuccessnet.com

Find living and nonliving things in the picture.

Count the living things. Write the number.

Count the nonliving things. Write the number.

Living Things	Nonliving Things

Lab zone **Take-Home Activity**

Look around your home. List three living things you see. List three nonliving things you see.

Vocabulary

Which picture goes with each word?

1. living
2. nonliving

 A

 B

What did you learn?

3. What do plants need to live?

4. What do animals need to live?

5. What might happen if a living thing does not get what it needs?

6. Observe Tell two things about a nonliving object you see in your classroom?

Alike and Different

7. How are these birds **alike and different**?

Alike	Different

Test Prep

Fill in the circle next to the correct answer.

8. Which one is nonliving?

    Ⓐ a person

    Ⓑ a hat

    Ⓒ a dog

    Ⓓ a plant

9. Writing in Science Make a list of three things you need to live.

Dr. Sonia Ortega

Dr. Ortega is a marine biologist.

Read Together

Dr. Sonia Ortega liked to look for insects when she was young. When she grew up she wanted to learn more about other animals.

Now Dr. Ortega studies oysters in the Atlantic Ocean. She wants to know where oysters grow the best.

Lab zone Take-Home Activity

Look for animals near your home. Draw pictures of them.

Chapter 2
Habitats

You Will Discover

- how habitats are alike and different.

- how the needs of plants and animals are met in their habitats.

Discovery Channel School
Student DVD

online
Student Edition
sfsuccessnet.com

Where do plants and animals live?

habitat

forest

wetland

Chapter 2 Vocabulary

habitat page 31

forest page 31

wetland page 34

ocean page 36

desert page 38

ocean

desert

27

Explore Where do animals live?

Materials

yarn

picture cards

land

word cards

What to Do

1 Make 2 yarn circles.

2 Sort the picture cards.
Which animals live on land?
Which animals live in water?

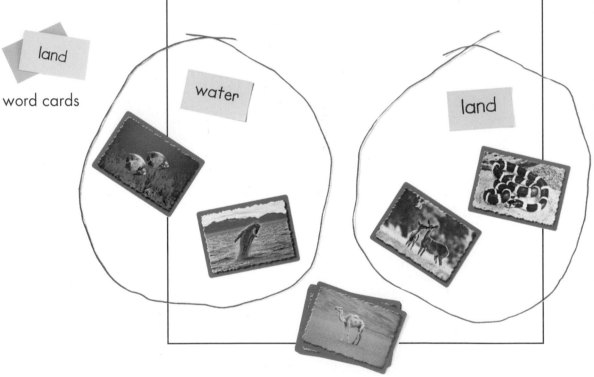

water

land

Process Skills

Sorting things is a way to show what you **observe**.

Explain Your Results
Observe the 2 groups.
Tell where each animal lives.

How to Read Science

Picture Clues

Pictures can give you clues about what you read.

Science Story

Grassland

These animals live in a grassland. The animals gather at the waterhole. The animals need water to live.

giraffe

grassland

Apply It!
Observe What lives in this grassland? Look for clues in the picture.

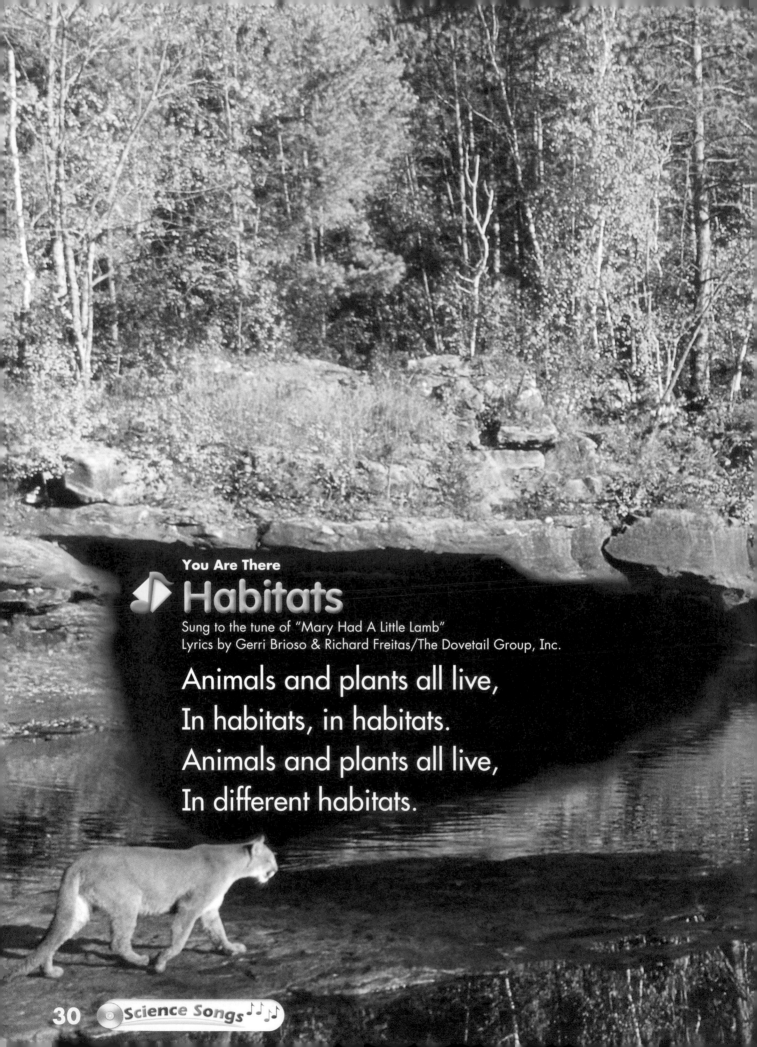

You Are There

♪ Habitats

Sung to the tune of "Mary Had A Little Lamb"
Lyrics by Gerri Brioso & Richard Freitas/The Dovetail Group, Inc.

Animals and plants all live,

In habitats, in habitats.

Animals and plants all live,

In different habitats.

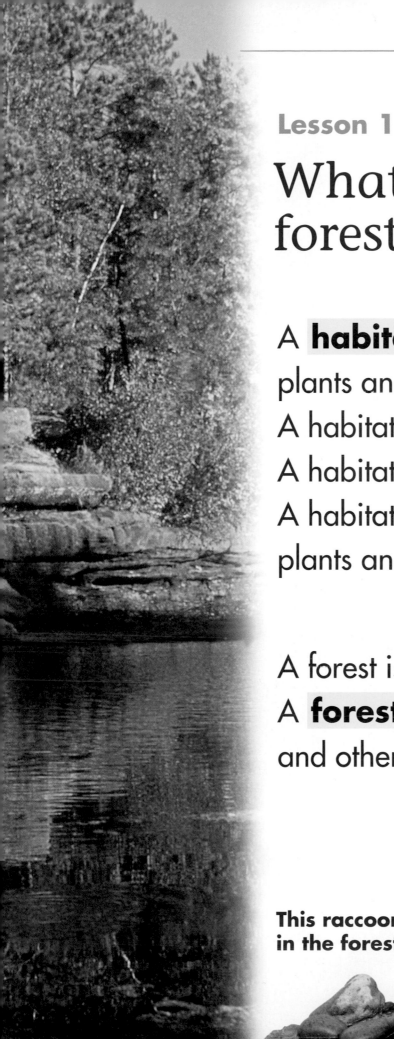

What is a forest habitat?

A **habitat** is a place where plants and animals live.
A habitat has food and water.
A habitat has air.
A habitat gives shelter for plants and animals.

A forest is a habitat.
A **forest** has many trees and other plants.

This raccoon lives in the forest.

Forest Plants and Animals

Look at the forest
in the summer.

Animals get the food
they need. Animals
get the water they need.

Plants get the sunlight
they need. Plants get
the water they need.

**This black bear lives
in the forest.**

32

winter

Look at the forest in the winter.

How does the forest change?

Plants get less sunlight. Many trees lose their leaves. It is harder for some animals to find food.

Map Facts
Superior National Forest is in Minnesota.

✓ **Lesson Checkpoint**

1. What is a habitat?

2. Use **picture clues** to tell how the forest changes.

33

What is a wetland habitat?

A **wetland** habitat is covered with water.
A wetland has food and water for animals.
A wetland has shelter for animals.

Look at this picture of a wetland.
Plants in this wetland get sunlight.
This wetland gets lots of rain in the summer.
This wetland gets less rain in the winter.
The winter is cooler than the summer.

This duck lives in a wetland.

Map Facts

A swamp is a wetland. Okefenokee Swamp in Georgia has about 70 islands.

crane

dragonfly

bullfrog

✔ Lesson Checkpoint

1. What does a duck get in a wetland?

2. 🔄 Use **picture clues** to tell what animals live in a wetland.

35

Lesson 3

What is an ocean habitat?

An **ocean** is a habitat.
An ocean has salt water.
An ocean is large and deep.

Many plants and animals live in an ocean.

Plants and animals get everything they need to live in their ocean habitat.

✓ **Lesson Checkpoint**

1. What is an ocean?

2. **Writing** in Science Write in your **science journal.** Write a sentence about living things in an ocean.

sea turtle

whale

fish

What is a desert habitat?

A **desert** is a habitat.
A desert is very dry.
A desert gets lots of sunlight.
A desert gets very little rain.
Many deserts are hot during the day.

Many animals and plants live
in the desert. The camel can live
without water for a long time.
The cactus can store water in its stems.

**This fennec fox stays
underground during
the hot desert day.**

Map Facts
The Sahara Desert is the largest desert in the world.

Africa

United States Desert

✓**Lesson Checkpoint**

1. What is a desert?

2. **Math** in Science Which thermometer shows the temperature of a desert during the hot day?

A

B

Investigate How do desert leaves hold water?

Materials

desert leaf shapes

water

waxed paper

What to Do

1 Wet the leaf shapes.

2 Fold the waxed paper over one leaf shape.

The waxed paper is like a waxy cover on a desert leaf.

3 Put both leaf shapes in a sunny place.

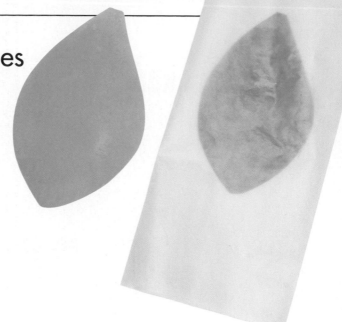

4 **Predict** Which leaf shape holds water longer?

	Predict	What happens?

Explain Your Results
Infer Why might a desert leaf have a waxy covering?

Go Further

What other question do you have about leaves? Plan a test to find the answer.

Math in Science

Counting Animals

forest

Make a tally chart.
Count the animals in the
forest picture.
Count the animals in the
desert picture.

forest	desert

Which of these pictures
shows more animals?

desert

Lab zone **Take-Home Activity**

Draw plants and animals in a
habitat. Are there more plants
or animals? Share your picture
with your family.

Vocabulary

Which picture goes with each word?

1. desert
2. forest
3. ocean
4. wetland

What did you learn?

5. What do these plants get from their habitat?

6. What does this deer get from its habitat?

7. Observe Describe a habitat near your school. What plants and animals live there?

Picture Clues

8. Use **picture clues** to tell about the wetland.

wetland

Test Prep

Fill in the circle next to the correct answer.

9. In which habitat might you see a camel?

Ⓐ desert

Ⓑ ocean

Ⓒ rain forest

Ⓓ wetland

10. Writing in Science Tell how a forest and a desert are alike and different.

Habitats at Kennedy Space Center

Kennedy Space Center is on Merritt Island. Kennedy Space Center is part of a wildlife refuge. A wildlife refuge keeps animals safe. This refuge has many habitats.

Florida

Map Facts
Merritt Island is in Florida.

Bald Eagles
Bald eagle nests on the wildlife refuge are safe.

Sea Turtles
Sea turtles lay their eggs on land. Their eggs are safe on the refuge.

Manatees
Manatees swim in the Banana River on the refuge. They are safe here.

Lab zone **Take-Home Activity**

Draw a picture of an animal that lives on Merritt Island. Tell your family about the animal.

Naturalists

Read Together

Naturalists study animals and plants.
Some naturalists help young cranes.
Some naturalists lead young cranes
to their winter habitat in Florida.
Now the cranes will know
where to go each winter.

This naturalist is leading cranes from Wisconsin to Florida.

Lab zone Take-Home Activity

Find Wisconsin and Florida
on a United States map. Tell
your family how naturalists
help young cranes.

EC NTL 10 9 8 7 6 5 4 3 2

You Will Discover

- parts that help plants and animals live in their habitats.
- parts that help living things keep safe.

Chapter 3
How Plants and Animals Live

online
Student Edition
sfsuccessnet.com

How do parts help living things?

flower

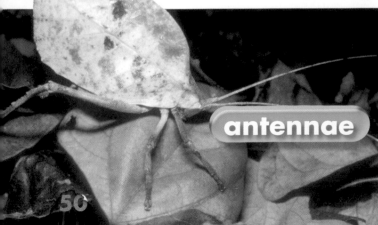

antennae

camouflage

Chapter 3 Vocabulary

antennae page 56

camouflage page 62

root page 68

stem page 68

leaf page 69

flower page 69

root

stem

leaf

51

Explore How can fur keep animals warm?

Materials

2 thermometers

2 plastic bags

cotton balls

tub with ice water

What to Do

1 Read the thermometers.

2 Put a thermometer in each bag. Add cotton balls to one bag.

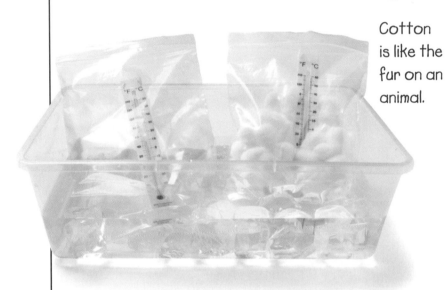

Cotton is like the fur on an animal.

3 Put the bags in ice water for 1 minute. **Predict** what will happen to each thermometer. Read the thermometers.

Explain Your Results
Communicate Tell how the thermometers show that fur can keep an animal warm.

Process Skills

When you **communicate**, you share what you know.

How to Read Science

TARGET SKILL
Alike and Different

Alike means how things are the same. Different means how things are not the same.

Science Pictures

Apply It!
Communicate

Tell how the foxes are alike and different.

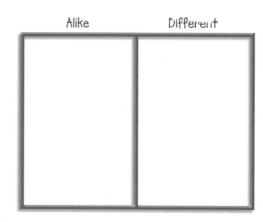

Alike	Different

You Are There

Something Special

Sung to the tune of "Froggie Went A Courtin'"
Lyrics by Gerri Brioso & Richard Freitas/The Dovetail Group, Inc.

It's very cold where the
    mountain goat lives, ah hmm.
It's very cold where the
    mountain goat lives, ah hmm.
But he has thick fur to keep him warm,
Even if there's a big snowstorm.
Ah hmm. Ah hmm. Ah hmm.

What helps animals live in their habitats?

Some animal body parts help animals live in their habitats.

These mountain goats live in a cold habitat. Thick fur helps keep the goats warm.

Hooves

Hooves help the goats climb on the rocks.

Living in the Ocean

This hermit crab lives in the ocean.
This hermit crab lives in a shell.
The hard shell helps keep the
hermit crab safe.

A hermit crab has antennae.
Antennae are feelers.
Antennae help the crab feel,
smell, and taste.

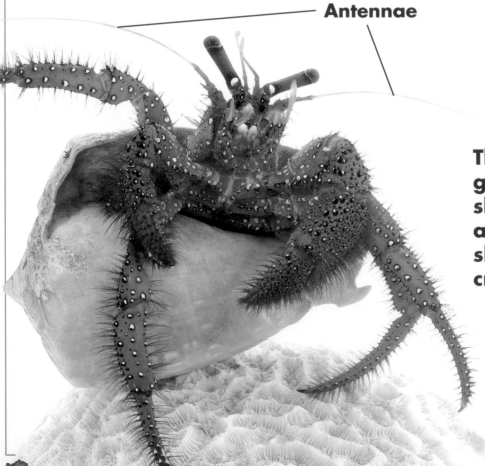

Antennae

The hermit crab
grew out of its
shell. Another
animal left its
shell. The hermit
crab moved in!

Swish! The clownfish uses fins to swim quickly in the ocean.

The clownfish uses a sea anemone for shelter.
A sea anemone is an animal.

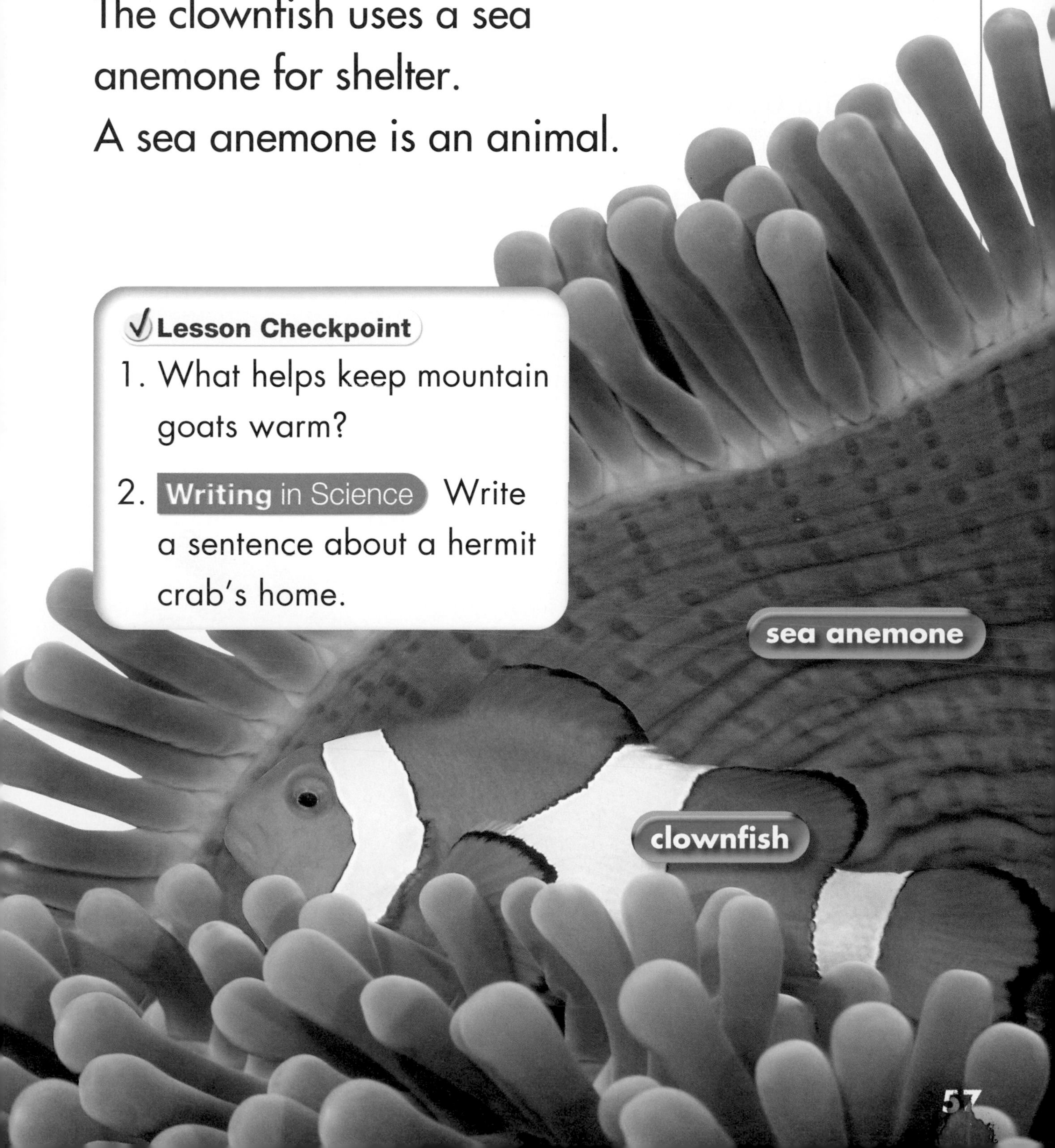

✓ **Lesson Checkpoint**

1. What helps keep mountain goats warm?

2. **Writing** in Science Write a sentence about a hermit crab's home.

sea anemone

clownfish

How do animals get food?

Animals use parts of their body to get food.

Birds fly to find food.
Birds use wings and feathers to fly.

Birds use beaks to eat food.
Crack! The cardinal's beak breaks seeds.
The owl's sharp beak tears meat.

Owl

Cardinal

Camels live in some deserts.
Food and water can be hard
to find in the desert.

A camel's hump has fat.
The fat helps the camel
live without food and
water for a long time.

1. ✓Checkpoint What part of a
camel helps it live in a desert?

2. 🎯 How are bird beaks
alike and different?

Other Ways Animals Get Food

A lion has long, sharp teeth for eating.

Whoosh! See the lion run. Strong legs help the lion run quickly.

The lion has good eyesight. The lion uses its nose to smell food. The lion's whiskers help it feel things.

A lion catches animals with its claws.

The lion tries to catch the zebra.

Look at the giraffes.
Giraffes have long necks.
Giraffes can reach
the leaves high in the tree.
Giraffes chew the leaves
with their flat teeth.

Giraffes eat
leaves.

☑ Lesson Checkpoint

1. What body parts help the lion
   catch food?

2. 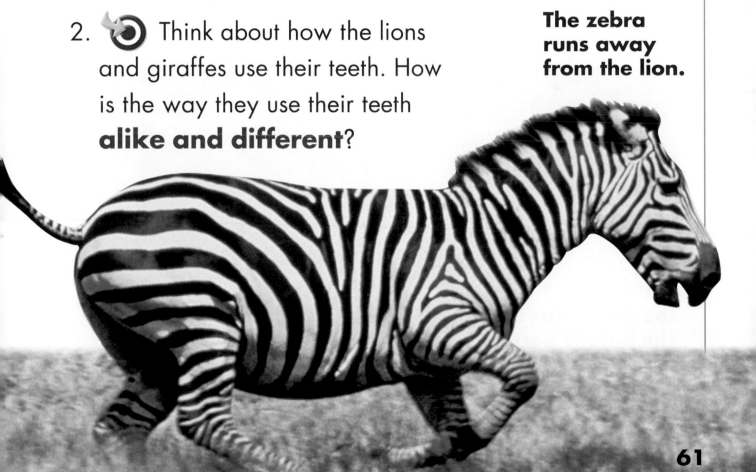 Think about how the lions
   and giraffes use their teeth. How
   is the way they use their teeth
   alike and different?

The zebra
runs away
from the lion.

What can help protect animals?

Camouflage is a color or shape. Camouflage makes an animal or plant hard to see.

Look at the snowshoe hares. Camouflage helps protect snowshoe hares.

The hare's fur is brown. The hare is hard to see in the woods.

The hare's fur changes to white. The hare is hard to see in the snow.

Can you find the katydid? Camouflage helps keep the katydid safe.

The katydid uses its antennae to find its way in the dark.

Earthworms live underground where they are away from the light. Heat and light dry out worms.

1. ✓**Checkpoint** How does the hare stay safe?

2. 🎯 How are the katydid and the hare **alike and different**?

Hiding in the Water

The crocodile lives in the water.
The hippopotamus lives in the water.

The crocodile and the hippopotamus
swim with only their eyes above the water.
It is hard for other animals to see them.

Crocodiles open their eyes under water. Special lids keep their eyes safe.

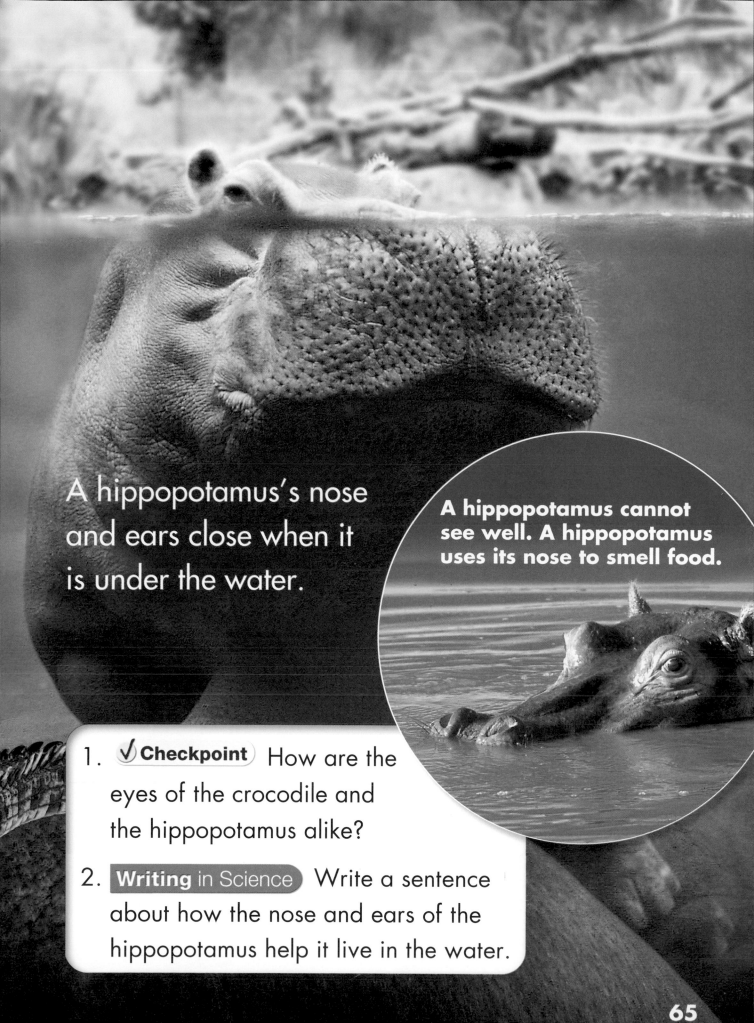

A hippopotamus's nose and ears close when it is under the water.

A hippopotamus cannot see well. A hippopotamus uses its nose to smell food.

1. ✓Checkpoint How are the eyes of the crocodile and the hippopotamus alike?

2. Writing in Science Write a sentence about how the nose and ears of the hippopotamus help it live in the water.

Animals Warn of Danger

Danger is near. This deer lifts and waves its white tail. Other deer see this and run.

Kangaroos move their ears to hear sounds all around.

Thump! Danger is near. The kangaroo pounds the ground with its back legs. Other kangaroos hear this and jump away.

A peacock's loud call can mean danger is near.

Screech! Danger is near. The peacock makes a very loud call. Other peacocks know to hide.

✓ Lesson Checkpoint

1. How do deer warn each other of danger?

2. **Technology** in Science What sounds warn people of danger?

Lesson 4
What are some parts of plants?

You learned about parts of animals. What parts of plants help them live and grow?

The **root** takes in water. Roots hold the plant in the ground. The **stem** takes water from the roots. Stems carry water to parts of the plant.

This stem's sharp thorns keep hungry animals away.

Roots

Stem

  **SciLinks** Take It to the Net sfsuccessnet.com | keyword: root code: g1p68

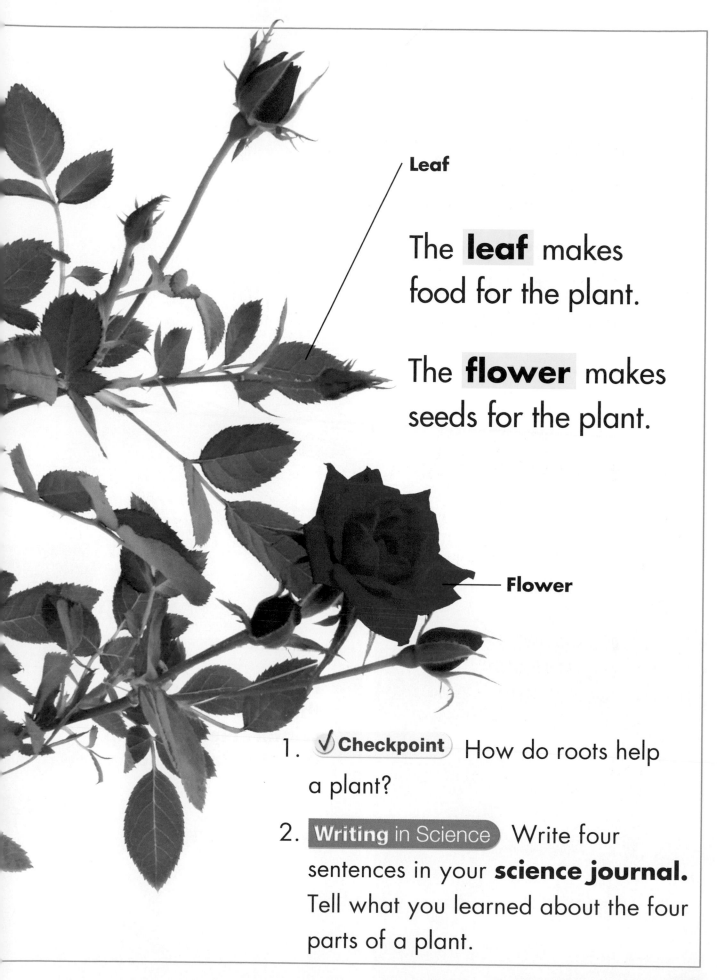

Leaf

The **leaf** makes food for the plant.

The **flower** makes seeds for the plant.

Flower

1. ✔Checkpoint How do roots help a plant?

2. **Writing** in Science Write four sentences in your **science journal.** Tell what you learned about the four parts of a plant.

Plants in Different Habitats

Look at the pictures.
These plants grow in different habitats.
These plants have different kinds
of leaves. The leaves have different
shapes and sizes.

Rain slides off this pointy leaf. This shape helps the leaf stay dry.

Wetland

Needles stay on the pine tree in winter. Needles help the pine tree hold water.

Forest

The sizes and shapes of leaves help plants live and grow.

✓ **Lesson Checkpoint**

1. What part helps the cactus live in the desert?

2. 🎯 How are the leaves of these plants **alike and different**?

Spines keep this cactus from losing water in the dry desert. Spines are leaves that look like needles.

Desert

Parts of the rain forest do not get much sunlight. Big leaves can take in more sunlight than small leaves.

Rain Forest

What helps protect plants?

Spines help some plants stay safe.
Spines keep some animals away.

Look at the spines on the thistle plant.

Spines

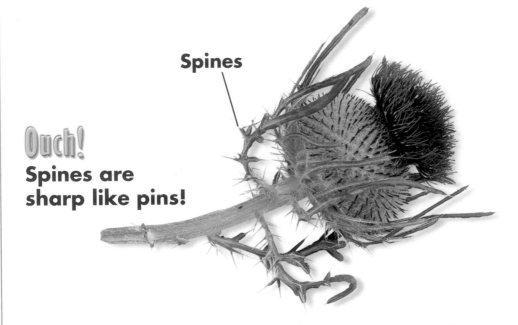

Ouch!
**Spines are
sharp like pins!**

Look at the flowers of the stone plants.
The flowers are hidden in the leaves.

These are stone plants.
Camouflage makes the plants hard to see.
Camouflage keeps the plants safe.
Their roots and stems are in the ground.
What you see are the leaves.

✓ Lesson Checkpoint

1. How do spines protect a plant?

2. **Math** in Science   Can you see more thistle plants or more stone plants on these pages?

Guided Inquiry

Investigate Which leaf shape drips faster?

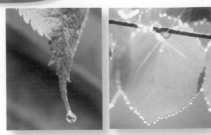

Materials

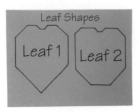

leaf shapes

scissors

tub with water

What to Do

1 Cut out the leaf shapes.

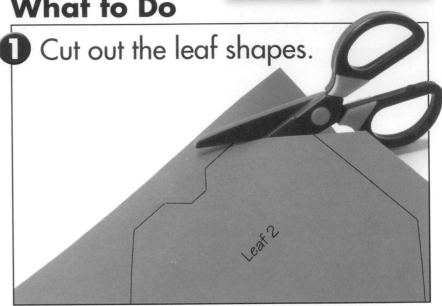

2 Dip the leaf shapes in water.

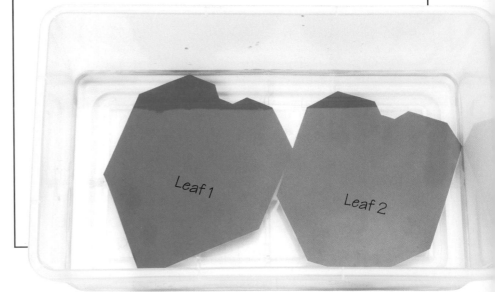

Process Skills

Observing your leaf shapes helps you learn why their shape matters.

3 Hold up your leaf shapes over the tub.

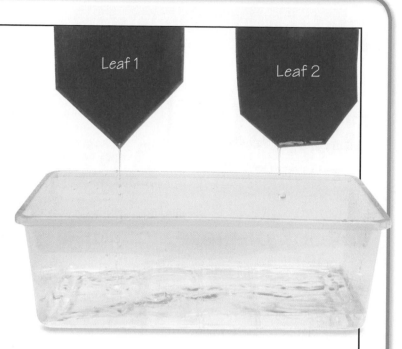

Leaf 1

Leaf 2

4 **Observe** how your leaf shapes drip.

5 Record in the chart.

Leaf Shapes	Fast or Slow Dripping
Leaf 1	
Leaf 2	

Explain Your Results
1. Which leaf shape drips faster?
2. **Infer** Which shape would help a real leaf dry off faster? Why?

Go Further
What would happen if you use 2 real leaves? Try it and find out.

Classify Animals

Look at these animals.
These animals can be sorted
in different ways.

Ways to Sort Animals

Animal	Fur or Feathers	Wings or No Wings	Teeth or Beak
lion	fur	no wings	sharp teeth
owl	feathers	wings	beak
giraffe	fur	no wings	flat teeth
cardinal	feather	wings	beak
rabbit	fur	no wings	teeth
deer	fur	no wings	teeth
kangaroo	fur	no wings	teeth

Use the chart to answer these questions.

1. What kind of body covering does an owl have?
2. Do more of these animals move with wings or no wings?

Take-Home Activity

Draw three different animals. Make a chart to classify them by size and by color.

Vocabulary

Which picture goes with each word?

1. antennae
2. camouflage
3. leaf
4. root
5. stem
6. flower

What did you learn?

7. What are three different ways animals move?

8. How do the parts of a plant help it grow?

9. What parts of a plant help protect it from animals?

10. Communicate Tell how the shape of a leaf can help water drip off it.

 **Alike and Different**

11. How are these plants **alike and different**?

Alike	Different

Test Prep

Fill in the circle next to the correct answer.

12. What part of a plant makes seeds?

Ⓐ stem

Ⓑ flower

Ⓒ root

Ⓓ leaf

13. **Writing** in Science Write a sentence about how camouflage helps keep living things safe.

Medical Researcher

Read Together

Dr. Todd Schlegel and Dr. Jude DePalma worked at NASA to create a machine that helps doctors see how astronauts' hearts work.

Doctors can use the machine to see if astronauts' hearts work the same way on Earth and in space. If doctors see that an astronaut's heart is having problems in space, then they will be able to help the astronaut get better.

Dr. Schlegel is looking for ways to help astronauts who have medical problems while they are on long trips into space.

Dr. DePalma wants the heart machine to help doctors all over the world too.

Lab zone Take-Home Activity

Draw a picture of how you help people. Share your picture with your family.

Chapter 4
Life Cycles

You Will Discover

- how animals change as they grow.
- how plants change as they grow.

online
Student Edition
sfsuccessnet.com

How do animals and plants grow and change?

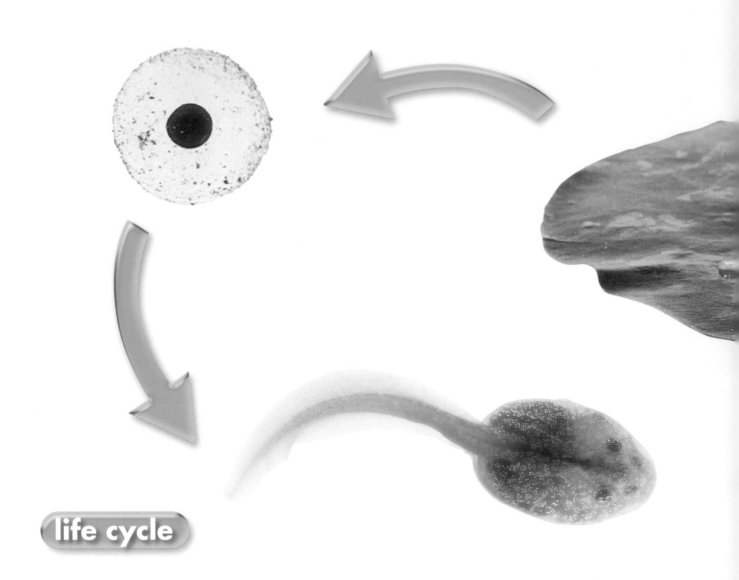

life cycle

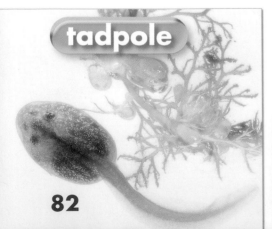

tadpole

larva

82

Chapter 4 Vocabulary

tadpole page 87

life cycle page 90

larva page 92

pupa page 92

seed coat page 98

seedling page 98

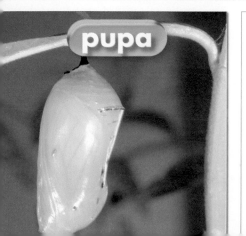

pupa

seed coat

seedling

Explore How do mealworms change as they grow?

Materials

home with mealworms

hand lens

What to Do

1 Use your hand lens. Observe the mealworms every day.

2 Draw and write about the mealworms.

They are alive! Handle with care.

Process Skills

When you **communicate**, you tell what you observe.

Explain Your Results
Communicate Tell how the mealworms change.

How to Read Science

 Put Things in Order

To put things in order means to tell what happens first, next, and last.

Science Pictures

Apply It!

Look at the pictures. **Communicate**
Tell which one comes first, next, and last.

First	Next	Last

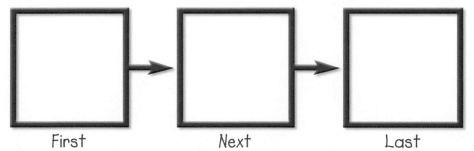

85

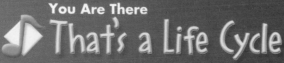

You Are There
That's a Life Cycle

Sung to the tune of "Pop Goes the Weasel"
Lyrics by Gerri Brioso & Richard Freitas/The Dovetail Group, Inc.

Let's play a game of "First, Next, Last"
So all of us will know,
How things change before our eyes
As they grow and grow.

Lesson 1

How does a frog grow?

The frog begins as an egg.
The frog egg hatches.
Out swims a tadpole!
A **tadpole** is a very young frog.

A frog egg is tiny. The egg feels like jelly.

A tadpole has a tail. A tadpole lives in water.

Tadpole

The tadpole swims in water.
The tadpole grows and changes.

This tadpole is five weeks old. Its back legs begin to grow.

Now the tadpole is nine weeks old. Its front legs begin to grow.

The young frog is still growing. Its legs are getting stronger. Soon the young frog will be a grown frog.

This young frog is twelve weeks old. Its tail is getting smaller.

1. ✓**Checkpoint** How does a tadpole change as it grows?

2. **Math** in Science Make a time line of the growing frog. Draw when it is an egg and how it looks at 5, 9, and 12 weeks old.

Grown Frog

The tadpole grows into a frog.
The grown frog lives on
land and in water.
The frog hops on land.

Animals grow and change.
All of these changes are
called a **life cycle.**
Look at all the changes
in the frog's life cycle.

**First, a frog starts
life as an egg.**

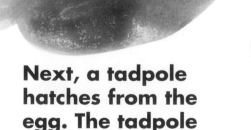

**Next, a tadpole
hatches from the
egg. The tadpole
swims in the water.**

Last, the tadpole grows into a frog. The grown frog may lay eggs in the water.

✓ **Lesson Checkpoint**

1. How do frogs and tadpoles move?

2. 🔄 **Put Things in Order**
   Tell about the life cycle of a frog.
   What happens first, next, and last?

How does a butterfly grow?

The butterfly begins as an egg. A larva hatches from the egg. A **larva** is a young insect. The butterfly larva is called a caterpillar.

A caterpillar becomes a **pupa** when it is changing inside a hard covering. Out flies a grown butterfly.

First, the butterfly is a tiny egg.

Next, the butterfly becomes a caterpillar. A caterpillar is a butterfly larvae.

92

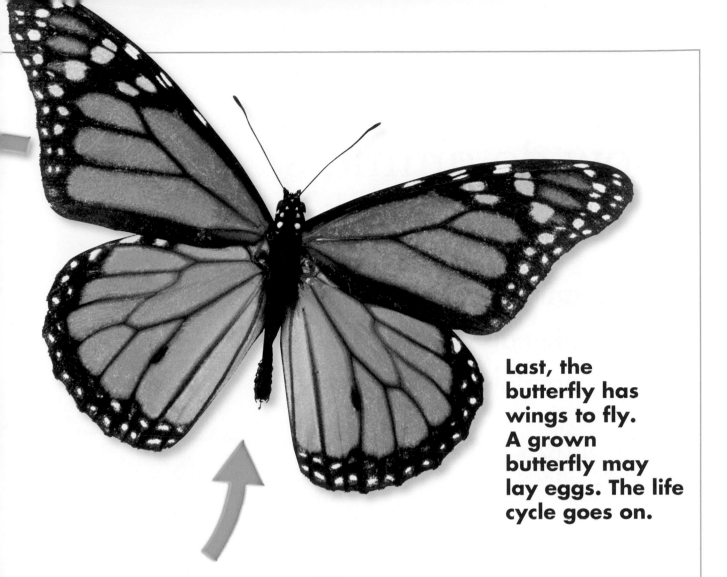

Last, the butterfly has wings to fly. A grown butterfly may lay eggs. The life cycle goes on.

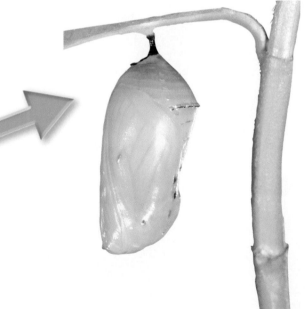

Then, the larva changes into a pupa.

✓ **Lesson Checkpoint**

1. What is a larva?

2. **Math** in Science How many steps are there in the life cycle of a butterfly?

How do animals grow and change?

Young animals change as they grow.
Young animals change size.
Young animals change shape.

Look at how the salamander changes.

The young salamander lives in water.

The grown salamander lives on land. How are the young salamander and the grown salamander different?

94

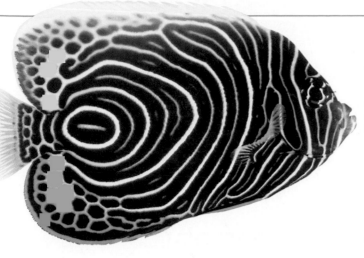

The young angelfish has spots and swirls. Its pattern will change.

The grown angelfish has a pattern of lines. How are the young angelfish and the grown angelfish alike and different?

1. ✓**Checkpoint** Tell two ways that animals may change as they grow.

2. **Art** in Science Draw and color a young angelfish. Draw and color a grown angelfish.

Growing Up

Young animals may look like their parents when they grow up. Will young animals look exactly like their parents?

Not always! Young animals may have a different color or pattern. They may be a different size.

Kittens will grow up to be cats.

A grown cat may have a different color pattern than its kittens.

One puppy may grow bigger than the other puppies.

The dogs are different colors. The dogs are different sizes.

Lesson Checkpoint

1. How do animals look different from their parents?

2. **Writing** in Science Write two sentences about how these dogs and puppies look **alike and different**.

How does a daisy grow?

Plants have a life cycle.
Most plants grow from seeds.
A **seed coat** covers the seed.
A seed coat protects the seed.

A seedling will grow
from the seed.
A **seedling** is a
very young plant.

First, the life cycle of a daisy begins with a seed.

Next, a seedling begins to grow. The seedling has roots and a stem.

98

Last, the seedling grows into a plant with flowers. The flowers make seeds. The seeds may grow into new plants.

✓ Lesson Checkpoint

1. How does a seed coat help a seed?

2. **Put Things in Order** What happens first, next, and last in the life cycle of a daisy?

How do trees grow?

A tree grows from a seed.
A tree changes as it grows.
A tree takes many years
to grow.

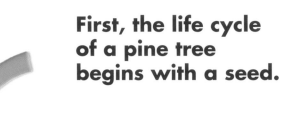

**First, the life cycle
of a pine tree
begins with a seed.**

**Next, a seedling begins
to grow. The seedling
has roots and a stem.**

Last, the seedling grows into a pine tree. The pine tree makes pinecones. The pinecones make seeds. The seeds may grow into new seedlings.

1. ✓Checkpoint What part of a pine tree makes seeds? How is this different from a daisy?

2. Writing in Science Write in your **science journal,** tell how a seed grows into a pine tree.

How a Cherry Tree Grows

A cherry is a fruit.
A cherry comes from a cherry tree.
The pictures show how
a cherry tree changes.

**First, it is spring.
The cherry tree has
many flowers. The
flowers lose their petals.
Cherries begin to form.**

Last, it is fall. Find the seed inside the cherry. A new cherry tree may grow from the seed.

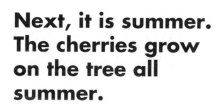

Next, it is summer. The cherries grow on the tree all summer.

✓**Lesson Checkpoint**

1. What will grow from the flowers on the cherry trees?

2. **Social Studies** in Science There are many cherry trees in Washington, D.C. Find this city on a map of the United States.

How do plants grow and change?

Young plants change as they grow. Look at how the tulip changes.

tulip seedlings

grown tulips

Tulips have different color patterns.

Tulips have different kinds of petals.

The oak seedling has a thin stem.
The oak seedling has
small leaves.
The oak seedling will grow.
It will start to look like the
grown oak tree.

oak seedling

The grown oak tree
has a thick trunk.
The grown oak tree
has big leaves.

grown oak tree

√ **Lesson Checkpoint**

1. How are the tulips alike
   and different?

2. **Art** in Science Find two leaves from
   the same kind of tree. Put them under
   paper. Rub the paper with a crayon.
   Tell how the leaves are different.

Investigate How do seeds change?

Materials

paper towels

cups

water

bean seeds

radish seeds

daisy seeds

What to Do

1 Fold a paper towel and put it inside a cup.

2 Ball up another paper towel and put it inside the same cup.

3 Wet the paper towels with water.

4 Put the bean seeds in the cup.

⑤ Repeat the steps with radish seeds. Repeat the steps with daisy seeds.

⑥ Observe the seeds for 10 days.
Collect Data Draw what you see.

Seed Changes			
	Bean	**Radish**	**Daisy**
Day 1			
Day 2			
Day 3			

Explain Your Results

1. What changes did you see in the different seeds?

2. **Infer** If you planted radish seeds and bean seeds in your garden, which would grow first?

Go Further
How would the seeds grow in soil? Make a plan to find out.

Comparing Size and Age

As people grow, their size changes. The girl in this picture has grown.

The table shows how tall the girl was when she was two, six, and ten years old.

Age	Size
2 years old	2 feet tall
6 years old	4 feet tall
10 years old	5 feet tall

1. How old was the girl when she was two feet tall?

2. How many feet did the girl grow from when she was six years old to when she was ten years old?

Lab zone Take-Home Activity

Make a table. Show the age of each person in your family. Write the names of the people in order from youngest to oldest.

Vocabulary

Which picture goes with each word?

1. tadpole
2. larva
3. pupa
4. seedling
5. seed coat

What did you learn?

6. How is a larva different from a butterfly?

7. What is one way to guess what a young animal will look like when it is grown?

8. Plants and animals grow and change. What are all of these changes called?

9. **Collect Data** Find out how many people in your class have pets.

Put Things in Order

10. Look at the pictures. Tell which one comes first, next, and last.

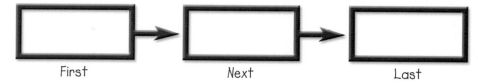

First   Next   Last

Test Prep

Fill in the circle next to the correct answer.

11. What is inside a pinecone?

     Ⓐ a daisy

     Ⓑ seeds

     Ⓒ needles

     Ⓓ a tree

12. **Writing** in Science Write a poem about how the cherry tree changes during the year.

Doctors

Read Together

Doctors help people stay healthy. People go to a doctor for a checkup. Doctors check people as they grow and change.

Doctors work to keep everyone in a family healthy.

The doctor will look at a person's eyes and ears. The doctor will listen to a person's heart. The doctor will ask people questions about how they feel. The doctor will answer questions too.

Doctors try to help sick people get well. The doctor might give a sick person medicine. Some medicines help a person feel better.

Lab zone Take-Home Activity

Make a poster. Tell some of the things that doctors do to help people stay healthy.

FC NT 10 9 8 7 6 5 4 3 2

You Will Discover

- that some plants make their own food.
- what animals eat for food.

Chapter 5

Food Chains

Web Games
Take It to the Net
sfsuccessnet.com

online
Student Edition
sfsuccessnet.com

113

How are living things connected?

food chain

oxygen

Oxygen is a gas in the air that plants and animals need to live.

rain forest

Chapter 5 Vocabulary

oxygen page 121

rain forest page 122

food chain page 125

marsh page 126

marsh

115

Lab zone Directed Inquiry

Explore What do animals eat?

Materials

matching cards

scissors

crayons or markers

glue

paper

What to Do

1 Cut out the cards. Color the pictures.

2 Match the cards. Show what each animal eats.

3 Glue the cards onto your paper.

Process Skills

You use what you know and what you observe when you **infer**.

Explain Your Results

Infer What kinds of things do animals eat?

How to Read Science

Draw Conclusions

You draw conclusions when you decide something about what you see.

Science Picture

The shark is looking for food.

Apply It!

Infer What do you think the shark will eat?

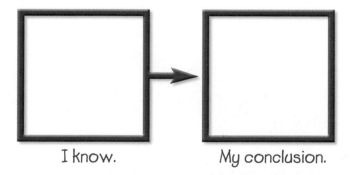

I know.   My conclusion.

Round and Round and Round

Sung to the tune of "The Wheels on the Bus"
Lyrics by Gerri Brioso & Richard Freitas/The Dovetail Group, Inc.

The plant uses sunlight
to make its food.
Make its food.
Make its food.
The plant uses Sun to make its food.
To grow and grow and grow.

How do plants and animals get food?

All living things need food.
Even you!

What do animals eat?
Some animals eat plants.
Some animals eat other animals.
Some animals eat plants
and animals.

Plants Make Food

Plants need food.
Leaves of green plants make food.
You might wonder how.

Roots take in water from soil.
The water goes up the stem
to the leaves.

Stem

Roots

— **Leaves**

Green leaves take in sunlight.
Green leaves take in air.
Green leaves use sunlight,
air, and water to make food.

Green leaves give off oxygen
when they make food.
Oxygen is a gas in the air.
Plants and animals need
oxygen to live.

✓ **Lesson Checkpoint**

1. Why are green leaves important
to plants?

2. 🎯 **Draw Conclusions** What
might happen to animals if plant
leaves did not give off oxygen?

121

How do living things get food in a rain forest?

A **rain forest** is a habitat.
A rain forest gets lots of rain.

The plant below grows in a rain forest.
The plant uses sunlight to make food.

The katydid eats the plant for food.
The lizard eats the katydid for food.

Crunch!
The katydid bites the plant.

Zap!
The small lizard will catch the katydid.

Swoop!
The bird will catch the small lizard.

The bird sees the lizard. The hungry bird eats the lizard for food.

1. ✔**Checkpoint** What does the katydid eat for food?

2. 🎯 **Draw Conclusions** What might happen to the bird if there were no lizards to eat?

Food for Animals

The hungry tayra spots the bird.
The tayra will catch the bird.
The tayra will eat the bird for food.

Pounce!
**The tayra will
leap at the bird.**

The plant makes food.
The katydid eats the plant.
The lizard eats the katydid.
The bird eats the lizard.
The tayra eats the bird.

This is called a **food chain.**
All living things are connected
through food chains.

Tayra

Bird

Lizard

Katydid

**Plant takes
in sunlight**

✓ **Lesson Checkpoint**

1. What does the tayra eat for food?

2. **Writing** in Science Write a sentence
   about the food chain in a rain forest.

Lesson 3

How do living things get food in a marsh?

There are food chains in a marsh. A **marsh** is a wetland habitat.

The marsh plant uses sunlight to make food. The rat will eat the plant for food.

126

The hungry snake slithers toward the rat.
The snake will eat the rat for food.

Gulp!
The snake will catch the rat.

1. ✓Checkpoint How are the plant and the rat connected?

2. Writing in Science Write a sentence about an animal in the marsh. Tell how it gets food.

Finding Food

The bird is hungry.
The bird sees the snake.
The bird will fly down
and catch the snake.
The bird will eat the snake.

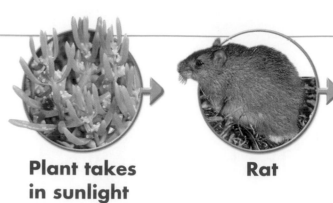

Plant takes in sunlight

Rat

128

Snake   Bird

The plant uses sunlight
to make food.
The rat eats the plant.
The snake eats the rat.
The bird eats the snake.
This is one kind of food chain
in a marsh.

Nibble, nibble!
**The bird will eat
the snake for food.**

✓ **Lesson Checkpoint**

1. How do animals in a marsh
   get food?

2. **Math** in Science   Put the marsh
   food chain in order. Use words
   such as *first* and *second.*

129

Investigate How can you make a model of a food chain?

Materials

crayons or markers

paper plates

tape

yarn

What to Do

1 Draw the plant. Show the sun in your drawing.

2 Draw the rat, snake, and bird from the marsh.

Process Skills

You use what you learn to **make a definition** of a food chain.

3 Make a model of a food chain. Connect your drawings with tape and yarn.

Label your food chain.

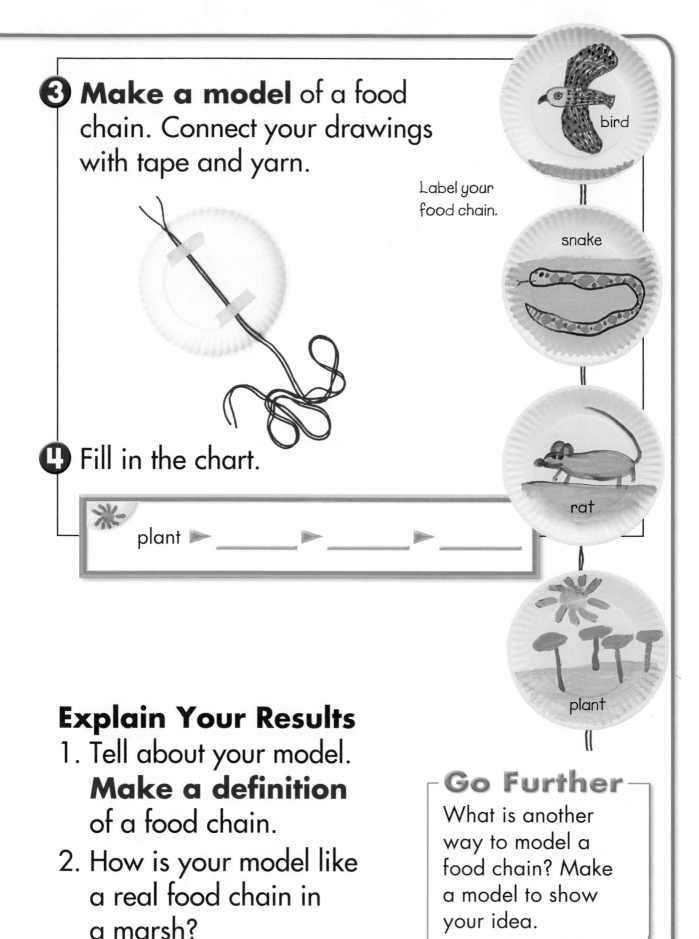

bird

snake

rat

plant

4 Fill in the chart.

plant ▶ _____ ▶ _____ ▶ _____

Explain Your Results

1. Tell about your model. **Make a definition** of a food chain.

2. How is your model like a real food chain in a marsh?

Go Further

What is another way to model a food chain? Make a model to show your idea.

Grouping Animals

Look at the Venn diagram.
It groups animals by what they eat.

e Tools Take It to the Net
sfsuccessnet.com

Grouping Animals by What They Eat

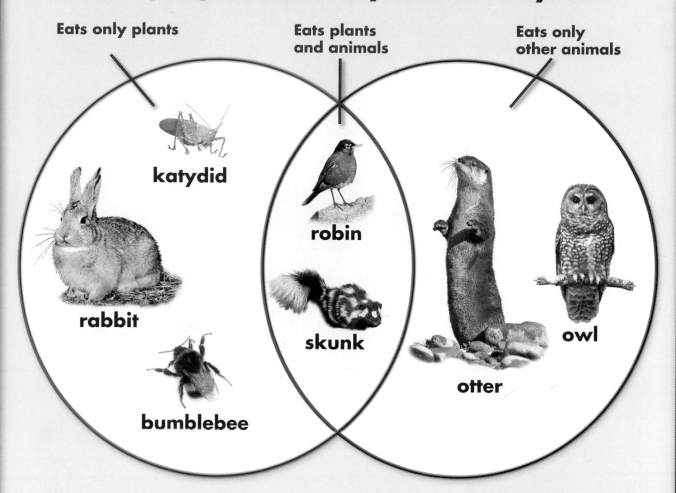

Eats only plants

Eats plants and animals

Eats only other animals

katydid

rabbit

bumblebee

robin

skunk

otter

owl

Use the Venn diagram to answer the questions.
1. How many of these animals eat only plants?
2. How many animals eat both plants and animals?
3. How many animals eat only other animals?

Lab zone Take-Home Activity

Find pictures of animals. Work with someone in your family to sort the animals. Make a Venn diagram that shows what the animals eat.

Vocabulary

Which picture goes with each word?

1. food chain

2. rain forest

3. marsh

What did you learn?

4. What is oxygen?

5. What do animals eat?

6. How are all living things connected?

7. Make a definition of a marsh using what you learned in this chapter.

Draw Conclusions

8. What do you think the bear will eat? **Draw conclusions.**

| I know. | My conclusion. |

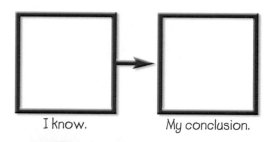

The bear is looking for food.

Test Prep

Fill in the circle next to the correct answer.

9. What is one kind of wetland habitat?

Ⓐ meadow

Ⓑ desert

Ⓒ marsh

Ⓓ forest

10. **Writing in Science** What do leaves use to make food? Make a list.

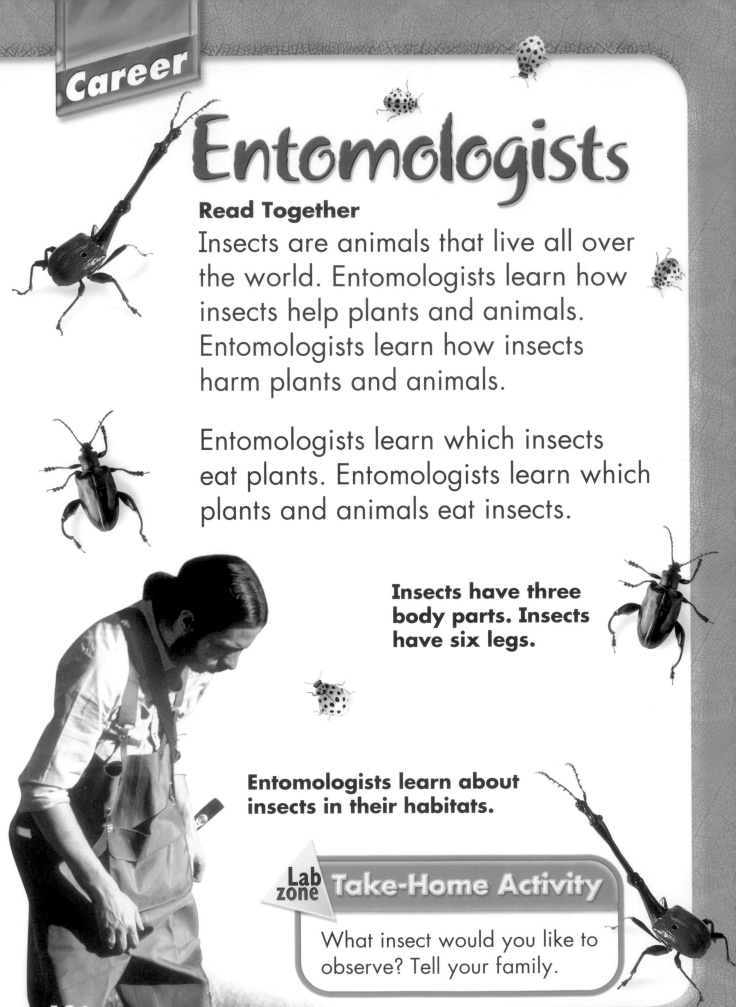

Entomologists

Read Together

Insects are animals that live all over the world. Entomologists learn how insects help plants and animals. Entomologists learn how insects harm plants and animals.

Entomologists learn which insects eat plants. Entomologists learn which plants and animals eat insects.

Insects have three body parts. Insects have six legs.

Entomologists learn about insects in their habitats.

Lab zone Take-Home Activity

What insect would you like to observe? Tell your family.

Unit A Test Talk

Find Important Words

Read the story.

Mark saw a squirrel in his yard.
The squirrel was eating seeds.
The squirrel was hiding seeds too.

Read the question.

1. What was the squirrel eating?

Ⓐ leaves

Ⓑ seeds

Ⓒ yard

Ⓓ hiding

Find important words in the question.
Find important words in the story that match
the words in the question. Answer the question.

137

Unit A Wrap-Up

Chapter 1

What do living things need?
- Plants need air, water, sunlight, and space to live.
- Animals need food, water, and shelter.

Chapter 2

Where do plants and animals live?
- Plants and animals live in different habitats.

Chapter 3

How do parts help living things?
- Different parts help animals get food and live in their habitats.
- Different parts help plants get water and make food in their habitats.

Chapter 4

How do animals and plants grow and change?
- Animals and plants grow and change in different ways. These changes are called a life cycle.

Chapter 5

How are living things connected?
- Living things are connected through food chains.

Performance Assessment

Make a Model Using Camouflage

- Make a model of an animal.
- Use camouflage on your model.
- Hide your model in your classroom.
- Tell how the camouflage made the model hard to see.

Read More About Life Science!

Look for books like these in your library.

Experiment How can camouflage help mice stay hidden from hawks?

Model camouflage. White beans are the field where mice live. Black beans are black mice. Beans with spots are white mice.

Materials

3 bags of beans

paper plate

timer

Ask a question.
How can camouflage help some mice stay hidden from hawks?

Make a hypothesis.
Are white beans with spots or black beans easier to see on a white background?

Plan a fair test.
Use the same number of black beans and white beans with spots.

Do your test.

1 One person is the hawk. The hawk must turn away.

2 Put the white beans on the plate. Add 10 black beans and 10 white beans with spots. Mix the beans.

3 Let the hawk turn around and pick up mice with one hand.

4 Take turns being the hawk. Record how many beans you pick up.

Listen for "Go" and "Stop."

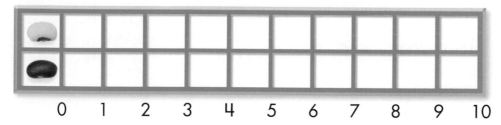

Mice   Field

Collect and record data.

Number of beans

	0	1	2	3	4	5	6	7	8	9	10

Tell your conclusion.
Which beans were harder to see? Which mice are harder to see in a white habitat?

Go Further
What if you added red beans? Experiment to find out.

The Frog on the Log

by Ilo Orleans

There once
Was a green
　　Little frog, frog, frog—

Who played
In the wood
　　On a log, log, log!

A screech owl
Sitting
　　In a tree, tree, tree—

Came after
The frog
    With a scree, scree, scree!

When the frog
Heard the owl—
    In a flash, flash, flash—

He leaped
In the pond
    With a splash, splash, splash!

Idea 1
Growing Plants in Soil

Plan a project.
Find out which kind
of soil is best for plants.

Using Scientific Methods
1. Ask a question.
2. Make a hypothesis.
3. Plan a fair test.
4. Do your test.
5. Collect and record data.
6. Tell your conclusion.
7. Go further.

Idea 2
What Birds Eat

Plan a project.
Find out which
kinds of foods
birds like.

FC NTL 10 9 8 7 6 5 4 3 2

Metric and Customary Measurement

Science uses the metric system to measure things. Metric measurement is used around the world. Here is how different metric measurements compare to customary measurement.

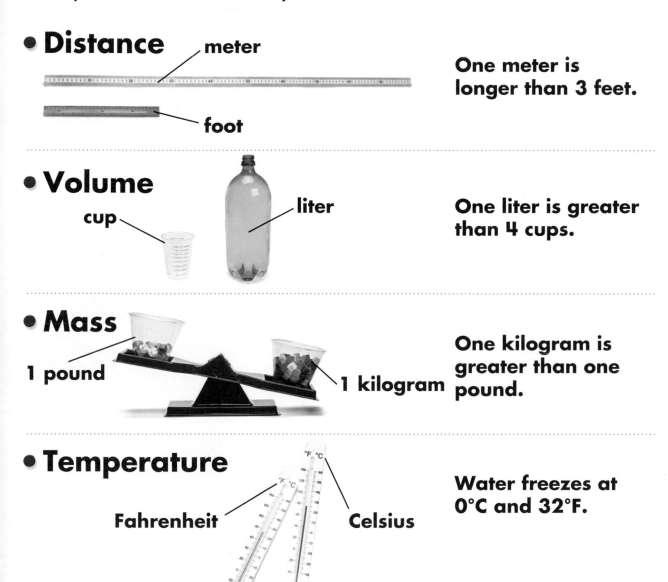

- **Distance**

meter

foot

One meter is longer than 3 feet.

- **Volume**

cup

liter

One liter is greater than 4 cups.

- **Mass**

1 pound

1 kilogram

One kilogram is greater than one pound.

- **Temperature**

Fahrenheit

Celsius

Water freezes at 0°C and 32°F.

Glossary

The glossary uses letters and signs to show how words are pronounced. The mark ′ is placed after a syllable with a primary or heavy accent. The mark ′ is placed after a syllable with a secondary or lighter accent.

To hear these words pronounced, listen to the AudioText CD.

A

alike (ə līk′) How things are the same. The two foxes look **alike**. (pages 5, 53, 213)

antennae (an ten′ē) Feelers that help some animals know what is around them. **Antennae** help the crab feel, smell, and taste. (page 56)

Antennae

attract (ə trakt′) Attract means to pull toward. Magnets **attract** some objects. (page 256)

B

battery (bat′ər ē) Something that stores energy. The toy robot uses a **battery** to move. (page 293)

C

camouflage (kam′ə fläzh) A color or shape that makes an animal or plant hard to see. **Camouflage** helps the rabbit stay safe in its environment. (page 62)

cause (kȯz) Why something happens. Taking out the bottom block can cause the tower to fall. (pages 245, 254)

clay (klā) A soft part of soil that looks like mud, is sticky when wet, and is hard when dry. The **clay** felt sticky when Tanya touched it. (page 156)

cloud (kloud) A form in the air made of many tiny drops of water or pieces of ice when water vapor cools. We watched the fluffy, white **clouds** float overhead. (page 186)

D

desert (dez′ərt) A desert is a very dry habitat that gets little rain. Many **deserts** are hot during the day. (page 38)

different (dif′ər ənt) How things are not the same. The dogs are different colors. (pages 5, 53, 96, 213)

dissolve (di zolv′) To spread throughout a liquid. Jenny stirred the lemonade to help the sugar **dissolve**. (page 225)

draw conclusions

(drò kən klü′zhənz) When you decide something about what you see or read. You can **draw** a **conclusion** about what the shark will eat. (pages 117, 277)

 E

effect (ə fekt′) What happens. The **effect** of pulling out the bottom block was that the blocks fell down. (pages 245, 254)

electricity (i lek′tris′ə tē) Makes things work. The streetlight uses **electricity** to shine. (page 290)

energy (en′ər jē) Something that can change things. Sunlight is a form of **energy** from the Sun. (page 282)

erosion (i rō′zhən) Happens when wind or water moves rocks and soil from one place to another. **Erosion** washed away the soil near the stream. (page 158)

evaporate (i vap′ə rāt′) To change from a liquid to a gas. The water on the ground quickly **evaporated** when the Sun came out. (page 228)

F

flower (flou′ər) The part of a plant that makes seeds. Our garden has many colorful **flowers**. (page 69)

food chain (füd chān) The way food passes from one living thing to another. All living things are connected through **food chains.** (page 125)

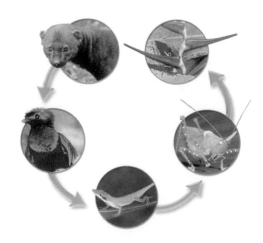

force (fôrs) A push or pull that makes objects move. The children used **force** to move the sled. (page 247)

forest (fôr′ist) A habitat with many trees and other types of plants. Many animals live in the **forest**. (page 31)

fuel (fyü′əl) Anything that is burned to make heat or power. People use gasoline as a **fuel** for cars. (page 290)

G

gas (gas) A kind of matter that can change size and shape. The bubbles are full of **gas**. (page 221)

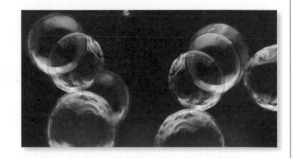

gravity (grav′ə tē) A force that pulls things toward the ground. **Gravity** pulls falling leaves toward the ground. (page 247)

H

habitat (hab′ə tat) A place where plants and animals live. A deer lives in a forest **habitat**. (page 31)

heat (hēt) Moves from warmer places and objects to cooler places and objects. The **heat** from the campfire kept us warm. (page 279)

humus (hyü′ məs) A nonliving material made up of parts of living things that have died. Grandmother adds **humus** to the soil to help her plants grow. (page 156)

important details (im pôrt′nt di tālz′) Pictures and words that tell you about something. We looked for **important details** in the book we were reading. (pages 149, 317)

inclined plane (in klīnd′ plān) A simple machine that is high at one end and low at the other. It helps move things up and down. The builders used an **inclined plane** to help move the wood. (page 359)

larva (lär′və) A young insect that has a different shape from the adult. A butterfly **larva** is called a caterpillar. (page 92)

leaf (lēf) A part of a plant that makes food for the plant. A **leaf** fell from the rose bush. (page 69)

lever (lev′ər) A simple machine that can be used to lift something. Denny used a **lever** to lift the nail out. (page 358)

life cycle (līf sī′kəl) The changes that take place as a plant or an animal grows and changes. The **life cycle** of a frog includes an egg, a tadpole, and a grown frog. (page 90)

liquid (lik′wid) Matter that takes the shape of its container. Water is a **liquid**. (page 220)

living (liv′ing) Things that are alive and can grow and change. The butterfly is a **living** thing. (page 7)

M

magnet (mag′nit) An object that attracts some kinds of metal. I put the note on the refrigerator with a **magnet**. (pages 256, 258)

marsh (märsh) A wetland habitat. My class saw many different plants and animals when we visited the **marsh**. (page 126)

mass (mas) Amount of matter in an object. Everything made of matter has **mass**. (page 215)

matter (mat′er) Anything that takes up space. Everything around you is made of **matter**. (page 215)

mineral (min′ər əl) A nonliving material that can be found in rocks and soil. Copper is a **mineral**. (page 164)

Moon (mün) An object in the sky that moves around Earth. The **Moon** was shining brightly in the night sky. (page 326)

natural resource (nach′ər əl ri sôrs′) A useful thing that comes from nature. Rocks are a **natural resource**. (page 155)

nonliving (non liv′ing) Things that are not alive, don't grow, and don't change on their own. Tables and chairs are **nonliving** things. (page 14)

ocean (ō′shən) A large, deep habitat that has salt water. Some fish live in an **ocean** habitat. (page 36)

oxygen (ok′sə jən) A gas in the air that plants and animals need to live. Most living things need **oxygen** to live. (page 121)

planet (plan′it) A large body of matter that moves around the Sun. Earth is one of the nine **planets**. (page 324)

pole (pōl) At the end of some magnets. The north **pole** of one magnet will attract the south **pole** of another magnet. (page 256)

predict (pri dikt′) To make a guess from what you already know. See the clouds high in the sky. What do you **predict** the weather will be like? (page 181)

pulley (pul′ē) A simple machine that uses a wheel and rope to move things up and down. The workers used a **pulley** to move the wood. (page 358)

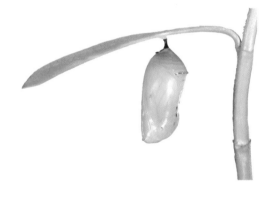

pupa (pyü′pə) The step after larva in some insects′ life cycle. The hard covering of the **pupa** protects the caterpillar while it changes into a butterfly. (page 92)

R

rain forest (rān fôr′ist) A habitat that gets a lot of rain. Plants with large green leaves grow in the **rain forest**. (page 122)

repel (ri pel′) To push away. The north poles of two magnets placed together will **repel** each other. (page 257)

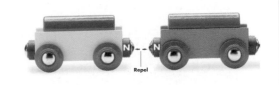

rocks (roks) Nonliving things that come from Earth. José collects **rocks**. (page 154)

root (rüt) Part of a plant that holds the plant in place and takes in water for the plant. We covered the **roots** of the rose plant with soil. (page 68)

rotation (rō tā′shən) The act of turning around and around. Earth's **rotation** causes day and night. (page 322)

S

sand (sand) Tiny pieces of broken rock. We made castles of **sand** at the beach. (page 154)

screw (skrü) A simple machine used to hold things together. A **screw** was used to keep the two wooden boards together. (page 358)

season (sē′zn) One of the four parts of the year. Winter is my favorite **season**. (page 192)

seed coat (sēd kōt) The protective shell that covers and protects a seed. The **seed coat** breaks open as the plant begins to grow. (page 98)

seedling (sēd′ling) A very young plant. Rafiq planted the **seedling** in his yard. (page 98)

shadow (shad′ō) A dark shape made when something blocks light. The doll made a **shadow** on the floor. (page 286)

shelter (shel′tər) A safe place for animals and people. This wolf pup uses an old log for **shelter**. (page 12)

simple machine (sim′pəl mə shēn′) A tool with few or no moving parts that does work. The wheel and axle of this wheelbarrow is a **simple machine**. (page 356)

sleet (slēt) Sleet is frozen rain. **Sleet** made the roads very slippery. (page 189)

solid (sol′id) A kind of matter that takes up space and has its own shape. A wooden block is a **solid**. (page 218)

speed (spēd) How quickly or slowly something moves. The car moved at a very fast **speed**. (page 250)

star (stär) A big ball of hot gas. **Stars** shine brightly in the night sky. (pages 319, 324)

stem (stem) The part of a plant that carries water to the leaves. The rose's **stem** has sharp thorns. (page 68)

Sun (sun) A big ball of hot gas that makes the day sky bright. The light from the **Sun** warms the Earth. (page 319)

tadpole (tad′pōl′) A very young frog. Rosie caught **tadpoles** in the pond. (page 87)

technology (tek nol′ə jē) The use of scientific knowledge to solve problems. A computer is a machine that uses **technology**. (page 343)

telescope (tel′ə skōp) Makes things that are far away look closer and brighter. We use a **telescope** to look at the stars in the sky. (page 324)

temperature (tem′per ə chər) How hot or cold something is. The **temperature** can be very hot in the desert. (page 184)

thermometer (thər mom′ə tər) A tool that measures temperature. We looked at the **thermometer** to see how cold it was outside. (page 184)

vibrate (vī′brāt) To move back and forth very fast. The banjo strings **vibrate** to make sounds. (page 260)

water vapor (wȯ′tər vā′pər) A form of water in the air. You cannot see **water vapor**. (page 186)

weather (weŦH′ ər) What it is like outside. I like to make snowmen when the **weather** outside is cold and snowy. (page 183)

weathering (weŦH′ər ing) The breaking apart and changing of rocks. **Weathering** can change the shape, size, and color of rocks. (page 158)

wedge (wej) A simple machine used to push things apart. The farmer used a shovel as a **wedge** to break up the soil. (page 356)

wetland (wet′land′) A habitat that is covered with water. Tanya saw a bullfrog when she visited the **wetland** near her home. (page 34)

wheel and axle (hwēl and ak′səl) A simple machine used to move things. A wheelbarrow has a **wheel and axle**. (page 356)

Index

This index lists the pages on which topics appear in this book. Page number after a *p* refer to a photograph or drawing.

A

Activities
　Directed Inquiry, Explore *See* Directed Inquiry, Explore.
　Full Inquiry, Experiment. *See* Full Inquiry, Experiment.
　Guided Inquiry, Investigate. *See* Guided Inquiry, Investigate.
　Take-Home. *See* Take-Home Activity.

Air, 13, 186, 221
　as natural resource, 160–161, 166
　heated, 279–280

Alike and Different, 5, 13, 17, 23, 53, 59, 61, 63, 79, 96, 97, 105, 213, 219, 221, 223, 237

Animals
　classifying, 76–77, 132–133
　food for, 58–61, 119, 124–135
　growth and change, 8, 81, 94–97,
　life cycles, 81–93
　as living things, 7–9
　needs of, 12–13, 119, 121. *See also* Habitats
　parts help in habitats, 54–65
　protection for, 52, 55–57, 62–67
　and soil erosion, 159

　sounds, 66–67, 264–265

Antennae, *p*50, 56, 63, 78

Apollo 11 (spacecraft), *p*334

Art in Science, 95, 105, 167, 287

Astronauts, 80, *p*238, 336

Attract, attraction, *p*242, 256–258

B

Batteries, 275, 293

Biographies
　Goldring, Winifred, 176
　Ortega, Sonia, 24
　Rahman, Shamim, 272
　Toro, Felix Alberto Soto, 304
　Wong, Mike, 368

Birds, 123–125, 128–129

Boiling, 227

Boulders, *See* Rocks.

Brine Shrimp, 18–19

Build Background, 2–3, 26–27, 50–51, 82–83,114–115, 146–147, 178–179, 210–211, 242–243, 274–275, 314–315, 338–339

Building technology, 352–356

Burning, 231

Butterfly, *p*7, 93

C

Camel, *p*39, 59

Camouflage, 62–65, 72–73, 78

Careers
　astronauts, 336
　doctors, 112
　entomologist, 136
　glassblower, 240
　medical researchers, 80
　meteorologist, 200
　naturalist, 48

Cars, 166, 290, 291

Caterpillar, *p*92

Cause and Effect, 245, 250, 255, 271

Chapter Review, *See* Reviews, Chapter.

Chihuly, Dale, 240

Classifying, 232–233, 237
　of animals, 76–77
　of plants, 364–365

Clay, *p*146, 156, 168–169, *p*172

Clouds, 186–187, 198

Collecting Data, 19, 106–107, 111, 140, 168–169, 173, 194–195, 204, 233, 308, 372

Color, and heat, 282–283

Columbia (space shuttle), *p*334

Communicating, 52–53, 79, 84, 85, 169, 194, 199, 212–213, 316–317, 340–341, 367

Compare, *See* Math in Science, Comparing.

Computers, *p*200, 304, 360, 368

Conservation, of resources, 163, 166

Controlling Variables, *See* Fair Test.

Corn, growing and harvesting, 344–347

Dairy, *p*294, 300, *p*301

Day and Night, 313–335, 322–323

Definitions, Making 130–131, 135

DePalma, Jude, 80

Desert, *p*27, 38–41, *p*44, *p*59, 71

Different, and Alike. *See* Alike and Different

Directed Inquiry, Explore, 4, 28, 52, 84, 116, 148, 180, 212, 244, 276, 316, 340

Dissolve, *p*211, 225

Doctors, 112

Draw Conclusions, 117, 121, 123, 135, 277, 281, 283, 303

Earth
surface of, *p*149, 151–152
making a model of, 149
rotation of, *p*315, 322–323

Effect, *See* Cause and Effect

Electricity, 290, 291, 292

Energy, 273–304
food as energy, 294–301
forms of, 274–275
heat, 279–281
and temperature, 282
using, 290–293

Engineer
aeronautical, 368
electrical design, 304

Entomologist, 136

Erosion, *p*146, 158–159

Estimating and Measuring, 194–195, 363

Evaporate, 211, 228–229

Experiment, *See* Full Inquiry, Experiment.

Explore, *See* Directed Inquiry, Explore.

Fair Test, plan a, 40, 204, 308, 372

Farmers, 345–347

Flowers, *p*50, 69, *p*73, *p*78, 98–99, 104–105

Food
for animals, 58–61, 118–119
cooking, 348–349
as energy, 294–301
growing, 344–347
liquids and solids, 224
for plants, 120
serving, 350–351

Food chains, 113–136
make a model of, 130–131
marsh, 126–129
rain forest, 122–125

Force, 247
magnetic, 259
and motion, 244–248

and sound, 260–261
and speed, 250–251
using, 248–249

Forest, *p*26, 31–33, *p*44. *See also* Rain Forest.

Fossils, 174–175

Freezing, 223, 226

Friendship (spacecraft), *p*334

Frogs, *p*35, *p*83, *p*91, *p*113
eggs, *p*90
growth of, 86–91
motion of, 90

Fuel, 290

Full Inquiry, Experiment, 140–141, 204–205, 308–309, 372–373

Fur, animal, 52–55

Gas, *p*210, 221, 227, 236

Geologists, 176

Glassblowing, 240

Goats, 54–55

Goldring, Winifred, 176

Graphs
bar graph, 196–197
picture graphs, 170–171, 300–301

Grassland, 29

Gravity, *p*242, 247, 252–254

Grow
and change, 6–8, 18–19, 94–97, 108–109. *See also* Life Cycles.

Guided Inquiry, Investigate, 18–19, 40–41, 74–75, 106–107, 130–131,

168–169, 194–195, 232–233, 266–267, 298–299, 328–329, 362–363

Habitats, 25–48
cold, 55
desert, *p*27, 38–39, 44, 59
forest, *p*26, 31–33, 44
grassland, 29
at Kennedy Space Center, 46–47
marsh, *p*115, 126–129
ocean, *p*27, 36–37, 44
rain forest, *p*114, 122–125
wetland, *p*26, 34–35, 44

Health in Science, 261, 295

Heat, 279
and energy, 282–283
from the sun, 276, 279
sources of, 279–281

Hill, 152

How to Read Science, xx-xxi, *See also* Target Reading Skills.
Alike and Different, 5, 53, 213
Cause and Effect, 245
Draw Conclusions, 117, 277
Important Details, 149, 317
Picture Clues, 29
Predict, 181
Put Things in Order, 85, 341

Human Beings, *See* People.

Humus, *p*146, 156–157, 168–169, 172

Hypotheses, Making, 140, 204, 308, 372

Ice, 226

Important Details, 149, 153, 158, 173, 317, 323, 327, 333

Inclined plane, *p*339, 358–359, 366

Inferring, 41, 75, 107, 116–117, 266–267, 271, 276–277, 299, 303, 329, 333

Insects, *p*7, *p*25, *p*50, *p*63, 92–93, *p*114, *p*118, *p*122, *p*125, *p*133, 136

Interpreting Data, 18–19, 195

Investigate, *See* Guided Inquiry, Investigate.

Investigating and Experimenting, 140, 328–329

Journal, *See* Science Journal.

Katydid, *p*50, 63, *p*114, 122–125, 133

Kennedy Space Center, 46–47

Land, 28, 148–153, 164–165

Landsat, 174

Larva, *p*82, 92, 110

Leaves, *p*51, 69–71, 74–75, 78, 120–121

Lever, *p*339, 358, 366

Life cycles, 81–112
animal, 81–97
butterfly, 92–93
definition, 90
frogs, 87–91
growth and change, 94–109
plant, 98–107

Light, 276–279, 282–283
and shadow, 284, 286–289, 298–299
sources of, 279, 284–285

Liquid, *p*210, 220–221, 236
changing, 223, 226–229
definition, 220
mixing with solids, 224–225

Living Things, *p*2, 4–9, 20–22

Lizards, *p*115, *p*119, 122–125

Magnet, *p*242, 256–259, 270–271

Map Facts, 33, 35, 39, 46,196

Marine Biologist, 24

Mars, 325

Marsh, *p*115, 126–129

Marsh, *p*210, 215

Mass, *p*210, 215

Math in Science
classifying, 76–77, 364–365
comparing, 108–109, 234–235
counting and sorting, 20–21, 42–43, 73, 93, 157, 253
fractions, 231
grouping animals, 132–133

making a chart, 189
measuring, 9, 289
adding, 349
put things in order,
129, 155
pattern, 323
reading a calendar,
330–331
reading a picture graph,
170–171, 300–301
speed, 268–269
thermometer, reading, 39
time line, 89
using a bar graph,
196–197

Matter, 209–240
changing, 222–234
describing, 216–217
on the moon, 238–239

Mealworm, 84

Measure, 9, 289

Merritt Island, 46–47

Metals, 258–259

Meteorologist, 200

Minerals, p147, 164

**Models, Making and
Using,** 131, 148,
328–329, 362–363,
372–373

Moon, p315, 326–331

Motion and Movement
of animals, 9, 88, 90
forces of, 242, 244–245
of planets, 320–322
and sound, 260–267,
270
and speed, *See* Speed.

Musical instruments,
260–261

NASA (National
Aeronautics and Space
Administration),
Biographies, 176, 272,
304, 368

Careers, 80, 200, 336
Exploring the Sky,
334–335
Habitats at Kennedy
Space Center, 46–47
Matter on the Moon,
238–239
Satellites Help Scientist
Find Fossils, 174–175

Natural Resources, 155,
160–165, 171
recycling, 166–171

Naturalists, 48

Night, and day,
313–335

Nonliving things,
p3, 7, 14–18, 21–22

Observing, 4–5, 19, 23,
28–29, 45, 74–75, 84,
168, 180, 186, 244,
299, 329

Ocean, 24, p27, 36–37,
44

Ortega, Sonia, 24

Oxygen, 114, 121, 134

Paleontologist, 176

People
energy for, 294–301
growth and change,
108–109

Picture Clues, 29, 33,
35, 45

Pine Tree, p70, 100–101

Plain, 152

Planets, 315, 324–325,
333

Plants, 8
in different habitats,
70–73

and erosion, 158
in the food chain,
122–125
food for, 120–121
growth and change,
p157
life cycles, 98–105
needs of, 10–11, 32,
188, 320
parts of, 68–69, 98,
120
protection for, 70, 73

Poems
The Frog on the Log, 142
Merry-Go-Round, 310
Taking Off, 374
Wind, 206

Poles, magnetic,
256–257

Pollution, 166

Predict, 181, 186, 191

Predicting, 40, 41, 52,
180–181, 199, 212,
232, 244–245, 298

Pull, 244–246, 248–249,
257

Pulley, p339, 358–359

Pupa, p83, 92, p93, 110

Push, 241–246, 249, 257

Put Things in Order, 85,
91, 99, 111, 129, 155,
341, 347, 355, 367

Rahman, Shamim, 272

Rain forest, 122–125

Rain gauge, p185

Reading Skills, *See*
Target Reading Skills.

Record Data,
See Collecting Data.

Recycling, 166–171

Repel, 243, 257

Reviews, Chapter, 22–23, 44–45, 78–79, 110–111, 134–135, 172–173, 198–199, 236–237, 270–271, 302–303, 329–330, 366–367

Rocket Scientist, 272

Rocks, p146, 154–155, 158–159, 164, 172

Roots, p51, p68, 78, 120, 158, 159

Rotation, 314, 322–323

Rust, 230

Sand, p146, 154–156, 168–169, 172

Saturn, 325

Schlegel, Todd, 80

Science Fair Projects, 130, 208, 312, 376

Science Journal, 36, 69, 101, 163, 193, 229, 257, 285, 296, 320, 359

Science Process Skills
xxii-xxiii
classifying, 232–233, 237
collecting data, 19, 106–107, 111, 168–169, 173, 194–195, 233
communicating, 52–53, 79, 84–85, 169, 212–213, 316–317, 340–341, 367,
estimating and measuring, 194–195, 363
inferring, 41, 75, 107, 116–117, 266–267, 271, 276–277, 299, 303, 329, 333
interpreting data, 18–19

investigating and experimenting, 140, 328–329
making definitions, 130–131, 135
making hypotheses, 140, 204, 308, 372
making and using models, 131, 148–149, 328–329, 362–363, 372–373
observing, 4–5, 19, 23, 28–29, 45, 74–75, 84, 168, 299, 328–329
plan a fair test, 204,
predicting, 40–41, 52, 180–181, 199, 232, 244–245, 298

Screw, p339, 358

Seasons, the, 192–193, 197

Seed coat, p83, 98–100, 110

Seedlings, p83, 98, 100, p105, 110

Seeds, 4, 98–101, 103, 106–107, 345

Shadows, 286–289, 298–299

Shelter, 12–13
animals as, 57
in the ground, 188
from rain, 188
rocks as, 155

Shepherd, J. Marshall, 200

Simple machine, p338, 356–359, 367

Sky
daytime, 318–321
exploring, 334–335
nighttime, 324–327, 328–329

Skylab (spacecraft), p334

Sleet, 189, 198

Snake, p127, p128, p129, 188

Snow, 190–191

Social Studies in Science, 103, 264, 361

Soil, 120, 156–159, 168–169

Solids, p210, 218–219, 236
mixing with liquids, 224–225

Songs
Can I Go Outside and Play?, 182
Energy, 278
Habitats, 30
Is it Living? I'd Like to Know!, 6
Look Up High!, 318
A "Matter" of Lemonade, 214
Pull the Sled, 246
Round and Round and Round, 118
Something Special, 54
Technology Helps, 342
That's a Life Cycle, 86
Water, Air, and Land, 150

Sounds
city, 262–263
and force, 260–261
investigating, 266–267
of nature, 264–265
vibration, 260
of warning, 66–67

Space Shuttle, p46, p333, 334, p336

Space Station, International, p335

Speed, p242, 250–251, 268–269

Spirit (space rover), p335

Stars, 319, 324–325

Steam, 227

Stem, p51, 68, 78, 120

Sun, 276, p314, 317, 319–322

Sunrise and sunset, 322

Surface, of Earth, 151–153

Tadpole, p82, 87–91, 110

Take-Home Activities, 21, 24, 43, 47–48, 77, 80, 109, 112, 133, 136, 171, 175–176, 197, 200, 235, 239, 240, 269, 272, 301, 304, 331, 335–336, 365, 368

Target Reading Skills,
alike and different, 5, 17, 23, 53, 59, 61, 63, 79, 97, 105, 213, 219, 221, 223, 237
cause and effect, 245, 250, 255, 271
draw conclusions, 117, 121, 123, 135, 277, 281, 283, 303
important details, 149, 153, 158, 173, 317, 323, 327, 333
picture clues, 29, 33, 35, 45
predict, 181, 186, 191, 199
put things in order, 85, 91, 99, 111, 341, 347, 355, 367

Technology, 343
building, 352–356
communication, 360–361
farm, 343–347
in the kitchen, 348–351
logging machines, 352–356

Technology in Science, 67, 160, 185, 227, 263, 293, 351, 353, 357

Telescope, p315, 324–325

Temperature, 184, 194–195, 282
and heat, 223, 283

Thermometer, 39, 52, p178, 184, p198, 283

Tools. See also Simple Machines
exploring, 340
kitchen, 348–351

Toro, Felix Alberto, Soto, 34

Trash, recycling, 165–171

Trees, p70, p101, p167
harvesting, 352–356
life cycles, 100–101
using, 164, 165

Venus, 325

Vibrate, vibration, 243, 260

Vocabulary, 3, 27, 51, 83, 115, 147, 179, 211, 243, 275, 315, 339

Water, 28, 120
bodies of, 151–153
changing, 226–227
and erosion, 159
and land, making a model, 148
using, 162–163

Water vapor, 178, 186, 227

Weather, 177–200, 183–185, 189

Weathering, p146, 158–159

Wedge, p338, 356, p357

Weight, of matter, 234–235, 239

Wetlands, p26, 34–35, p44, 70. See also Marsh

Wheel and axle, p338, 356, p357

Wilson, Stephanie, 336

Wind, 167, 180

Wong, Mike, 368

Writing in Science, 11, 14, 23, 36, 45, 57, 65, 69, 79, 97, 101, 111, 125, 127, 135, 163, 164, 173, 193, 199, 216, 225, 229, 237, 249, 257, 259, 271, 285, 291, 296, 303, 320, 333, 345, 359, 367

Credits

Text

"The Frog on the Log" by Ilo Orleans from *Read-Aloud Rhymes for the Very Young* selected by Jack Prelutsky. Copyright ©1986 by Alfred A. Knopf.

"Wind" from *Some Folks Like Cats and Other Poems* by Ivy O. Eastwick. Reprinted by permission of Boyds Mills Press.

"Merry-Go-Round" from *I Like Machinery* by Dorothy Baruch.

"Taking Off" from *Very Young Verses*, edited by Barbara Peck Geismer and Antoinette Brown Suter. Copyright ©1945 by Houghton Mifflin company; Copyright ©Renewed 1972 by Barbara P. Geismer and Antoinette Brown Suter. Reprinted by permission of Houghton Mifflin Company. All Rights Reserved.

Illustrations

31-32, 34, 36, 38 Robert Hynes; 108-109 Cheryl Mendenhall; 322 Henk Dawson.

Photographs

Every effort has been made to secure permission and provide appropriate credit for photographic material. The publisher deeply regrets any omission and pledges to correct errors called to its attention in subsequent editions.

Unless otherwise acknowledged, all photographs are the property of Scott Foresman, a division of Pearson Education.

Photo locators denoted as follows: Top (T), Center (C), Bottom (B), Left (L), Right (R), Background (Bkgd).

Cover: (C) ©Tui De Roy/Minden Pictures, (Bkgd) ©Tim Davis/Corbis, (BL) Getty Images.

Front Matter: ii ©DK Images; iii (TR, B) ©DK Images; v ©DK Images; vi (B) ©DK Images, (CL) Corbis; vii Getty Images; viii (CL) Digital Vision, (BC) ©DK Images; ix (CR) ©Michael and Patricia Fogden/Corbis, (B) ©DK Images; x (TL, CL, B) ©Michael & Patricia Fogden/Corbis, (BR) ©Rick and Nora Bowers/Visuals Unlimited; xii (CL) ©Richard Price/Getty Images, (CL) ©Thomas Kitchin/Tom Stack & Associates, Inc.; xiii (CR) Stephen Oliver/©DK Images, (CR) Getty Images; xiv (CL) Getty Images, (B) ©DK Images; xv ©Frank Siteman/PhotoEdit; xvi ©Stone/Getty Images; xvii Courtesy of the London Toy and Model Museum/Paddington, London/©DK Images; xviii (CL) NASA Image Exchange, (CL) ©Roger Ressmeyer/Corbis; xix ©Lowell Georgia/Corbis; xx ©DK Images; xxii ©Douglas Faulkner/Photo Researchers, Inc.; xxiii ©William Harrigan/Lonely Planet Images; xxiv ©William Harrigan/Lonely Planet Images; xxv (BC) ©John Pontier/Animals Animals/Earth Scenes, (TR) ©Ames/NASA; xxix ©Ed Bock/Corbis; xxxi ©Little Blue Wolf Productions/Corbis; xxxii ©Andy Crawford/DK Images.

Unit A: Divider: ©Wayne R. Bilenduke/Getty Images; 1 (C) ©Sumio Harada/Minden Pictures, (TR) ©Royalty-Free/Corbis; 2 (B) Corbis, (T) ©Pat O'Hara/Corbis; 3 ©Mary Kate Denny/PhotoEdit; 5 (Bkgd) ©Pat O'Hara/Corbis, (C) ©Royalty-Free/Corbis, (TR) ©DK Images; 6 ©Pat O'Hara/Corbis; 7 (BR) ©Darrell Gulin/Corbis, (TR) ©DK Images; 8 (TR) ©Photowood, Inc./Corbis, (TL) Getty Images; 9 (TL) ©Manoj Shah/Animals Animals/Earth Scenes, (BR) ©J. & B. Photographers/Animals Animals/Earth Scenes; 10 (BL) ©Roy Morsch/Corbis, (TL) Digital Vision; 11 ©Guy Edwardes/Getty Images; 12 (BL) ©Darrell Gulin/Corbis, (C) Corbis, (TL) ©DK Images; 13 ©Dan Guravich/Corbis; 14 ©Mary Kate Denny/PhotoEdit; 16 (TL, C) ©DK Images; 17 Brand X Pictures; 22 (TC) ©Manoj Shah/Animals Animals/Earth Scenes, (B) ©J. & B. Photographers/Animals Animals/Earth Scenes; 23 (TR) ©Darrell Gulin/Corbis, (CL, C) ©DK Images; 24 (TL) Alan Schroeder/Courtesy of Sonia Ortega, (B) ©John Bova/Photo Researchers, Inc.; **Chapter 2:** 25 (C) Getty Images, (TR) ©Stephen Dalton/Photo Researchers, Inc.; 26 (C) ©W. Perry Conway/Corbis, (BL) ©Daniel J. Cox/Natural Exposures, (BR) ©David Samuel Robbins/Corbis; 27 (BR) ©Yva Momatiuk/John Eastcott/Minden Pictures, (BL) Digital Vision; 29 (Bkgd) ©W. Perry Conway/Corbis, (TR, C) ©DK Images; 30 ©W. Perry Conway/Corbis; 31 (BR) ©Taxi/Getty Images, (TR) ©Jeremy Thomas/Natural Visions; 32 (TL) ©Jeremy Thomas/Natural Visions, (BL) ©Jeffrey Lepore/Photo Researchers, Inc., (CR) ©Daniel J. Cox/Natural Exposures; 33 ©Daniel J. Cox/Natural Exposures; 34 (BC) ©Steve Maslowski/Photo Researchers, Inc., (TL) Brand X Pictures; 35 (C) ©David Samuel Robbins/Corbis, (BR) ©Joe McDonald/Corbis, (TR) ©Stone/Getty Images, (CR) Getty Images; 36 (CR) Digital Vision, (TL) ©Stone/Getty Images; 37 (CR) ©Flip Nicklin/Minden Pictures, (TR) Getty Images, (BR) ©Photographer's Choice/Getty Images; 38 (TL) ©Photographer's Choice/Getty Images, (BL) ©DK Images; 39 (BC) ©Yva Momatiuk/John Eastcott/Minden Pictures, (TC) ©Jose Fuste Raga/Corbis; 40 ©Yva Momatiuk/John Eastcott/Minden Pictures, (TR) ©Gerry Ellis/Minden Pictures; 42 (BC) ©Nigel J. Dennis/NHPA Limited, (T) ©Art Wolfe/Stone/Getty Images; 44 (TR, BR) ©Daniel J. Cox/Natural Exposures, (CL) ©David Samuel Robbins/Corbis, (CR) ©Yva Momatiuk/John Eastcott/Minden Pictures, (TR) Digital Vision; 45 (C) ©Robert Lubeck/Animals Animals/Earth Scenes, (TR) Brand X Pictures; 46 NASA; 47 (TR) Getty Images, (CL) ©Porterfield/Chickering/Photo Researchers, Inc., (BR) ©Doug Perrine/DRK Photo; 48 (BC) ©Operation Migration, Inc.; **Chapter 3:** 49 (TL) ©DK Images, (C) ©Michael Patrick O'Neill/NHPA Limited; 50 (BL) ©Richard K. LaVal/Animals Animals/Earth Scenes, (BR) ©T. Kitchin and V. Hurst/NHPA Limited, (C) Digital Vision; 51 (BR) ©Jeff Lepore/Photo Researchers, Inc., (BL) ©J.P. Ferrero/Jacana/Photo Researchers, Inc.; 53 (Bkgd) Digital Vision, (CL) Corel, (CR) ©Lynn Stone/Index Stock Imagery, (TR) ©Helen Williams/Photo Researchers, Inc.; ©54 David Fritts/Stone/Getty Images; 55 (BR) ©Steve Coombs/Photo Researchers, Inc., (TR) Getty Images; 56 (B) ©DK Images, (TL, C) ©B. Jones and M. Shimlock/NHPA Limited; 58 (TL, BL) ©Helen Williams/Photo Researchers, Inc., (BR) ©DK Images; 59 ©Noboru Komine/Photo Researchers, Inc.; 60 (CR) ©Mitsuaki Iwago/Minden Pictures, (TR) Digital Vision, (B) ©S. Purdy Matthews/Stone/Getty Images, (TL) ©Ana Laura Gonzalez/Animals

Animals/Earth Scenes; 61 ©Art Wolfe/Getty Images; 62 (BL) ©Stephen Krasemann/Stone, (CR) ©T. Kitchin and V. Hurst/ NHPA Limited, (TL) ©Richard K. LaVal/Animals Animals/ Earth Scenes; 63 (T) ©Richard K. LaVal/Animals Animals/ Earth Scenes, (B) ©J.P. Ferrero/Jacana/Photo Researchers, Inc.; 64 (BC) ©Dante Fenolio/Photo Researchers, Inc., (TL, BC) ©DK Images; 65 (C) ©John Warden/Stone/Getty Images, (CR) ©Tom and Pat Leeson/Photo Researchers, Inc.; 66 (CR) ©DK Images, (TL) ©Jerry Young/©DK Images, (CL) ©Virginia Neefus/Animals Animals/Earth Scenes; 67 ©Chase Swift/Corbis; 70 (BR) ©Tom & Pat Leeson/Photo Researchers, Inc., (CL) Getty Images, (TL, CR) ©DK Images, (BL) ©Alan and Sandy Carey/Getty Images; 71 (CL) ©John Eastcott and Yva Momatiuk/NGS Image Collection, (BL) ©Ed Reschke/Peter Arnold, Inc., (CR, BR) ©DK Images; 72 (TL, C) ©DK Images; 73 (C, CR) ©DK Images; 74 (TR) ©H. H./Getty Images, (TC) Getty Images; 76 (Bkgd) ©Arctic National Wildlife Refuge/Getty Images, (CR) ©Art Wolfe/Getty Images, (B) ©S. Purdy Matthews/Stone/Getty Images; 77 (CR) ©Virginia Neefus/Animals Animals/Earth Scenes, (TR, BR) ©DK Images, (CR) ©Stephen Krasemann/Stone, (CC) ©Helen Williams/Photo Researchers, Inc.; 78 (CR) ©J.P. Ferrero/Jacana/Photo Researchers, Inc., (BR) ©Darrell Gulin/ Corbis, (C) ©DK Images; 79 (C) Photo 24/Brand X Pictures, (CR) ©Ralph A. Clevenger/Corbis, (TR) ©DK Images; 80 (BL) ©JSC/NASA, (BR, Bkgd) NASA; **Chapter 4:** 81 ©Allen Russell/Index Stock Imagery; 82 (TL, C, BL) ©DK Images, (BR) ©Michael and Patricia Fogden/Corbis; 83 (BR) ©David Young-Wolff/PhotoEdit, (CR, BC) ©DK Images, (BL) ©George D. Lepp/Corbis; 85 (TR, C, CL) ©DK Images, (CR) Odds Farm Park/©DK Images, (Bkgd) ©Stephen Dalton/NHPA Limited; 86 ©Stephen Dalton/NHPA Limited; 87 (TR, CR, BR) ©DK Images; 88 (TL, C, B) ©DK Images; 89 ©DK Images; 90 (TR, B) ©DK Images, (TL) ©Geoff Brightling/©DK Images; 91 ©DK Images; 92 (T) ©George D. Lepp/Corbis, (B) ©Michael and Patricia Fogden/Corbis, (TL) ©DK Images; 93 (BL) George D. Lepp/Corbis, (T) ©DK Images; 94 (CR) ©T. Wiewandt/DRK Photo, (B) ©Joseph T. Collins/Photo Researchers, Inc., (TL) ©DK Images; 95 (TL) ©Jane Burton/ Bruce Coleman, Inc., (C) ©Norbert Wu/Minden Pictures; 96 (BL) ©Pam Francis/Getty Images, (CR) ©Pat Doyle/Corbis; 97 (TR) ©George D. Lepp/Corbis, (B) ©Bruce Ando/Index Stock Imagery; 98 Derek Hall/©DK Images; 99 ©DK Images; 100 (TL) Matthew Ward/©DK Images, (BL) ©David Young-Wolff/PhotoEdit; 101 (BR) ©Bill Ross/Corbis, (TC) ©DK Images; 102 (B) ©DK Images, (CL) ©A. Riedmiller/Peter Arnold, Inc.; 103 ©DK Images; 104 (CL, CC, CR) Brand X Pictures, (BL, BR) ©DK Images; 105 (TR) ©Stephen Dalton/ Photo Researchers, Inc., (B) ©Royalty-Free/Corbis; 106 ©Steve Terrill/Corbis; 110 (TR) ©David Young-Wolff/ PhotoEdit, (TC) ©George D. Lepp/Corbis, (CL) ©Michael and Patricia Fogden/Corbis, (TL, CR) ©DK Images, (BR) ©Nicolas Granier/Peter Arnold, Inc.; 111 (TR) ©DK Images, (CL, CR) ©Jeff Foott/Bruce Coleman Collection, (C) ©Daniel W. Gotshall/Seapics; 112 ©Ed Bock/Corbis; **Chapter 5:** 113 (C) ©Jonathan Blair/Corbis, (TR) ©David Aubrey/Corbis, (BC) ©Clive Druett/Papilio/Corbis; 114 (BR) ©Gary Braasch/Corbis, (C) ©Michael & Patricia Fogden/Corbis, (T) ©Ken Lucas/Visuals Unlimited; 115 ©Hal Horwitz/Corbis; 117 (C) Getty Images, (TR, Bkgd) ©Michael & Patricia

Fogden/Corbis; 118 ©Michael & Patricia Fogden/Corbis; 119 ©Michael & Patricia Fogden/Minden Pictures; 122 (B, BL) ©Michael & Patricia Fogden/Corbis, (TL) ©Michael Fogden/Animals Animals/Earth Scenes, (BR) ©Rick and Nora Bowers/Visuals Unlimited; 123 ©Kevin Schafer/NHPA Limited; 124 (TL) ©Michael & Patricia Fogden/Corbis, (BL) ©Kevin Schafer/NHPA Limited, (B) ©Steve Kaufman/Corbis; 125 (C) ©Rick and Nora Bowers/Visuals Unlimited, (CR) ©Kevin Schafer/NHPA Limited, (BR) ©Michael & Patricia Fogden/Corbis, (TR) ©Steve Kaufman/Corbis; 126 (B) ©Sue A. Thompson/Visuals Unlimited, (TL) ©Royalty-Free/Corbis; 127 ©David A. Northcott/Corbis; 128 (C) ©David A. Northcott/Corbis, (TC) ©Rick Poley/Visuals Unlimited, (TL) ©David A. Ponton/Mira, (TR) ©William J. Weber/Visuals Unlimited, (B) ©Sue A. Thompson/Visuals Unlimited; 129 (TC) ©Ted Levin/Animals Animals/Earth Scenes, (TL) ©Royalty-Free/Corbis, (CR) ©James Allen/Bruce Coleman, Inc.; 132 (TC) ©Michael & Patricia Fogden/Corbis, (C) ©John Shaw/Tom Stack & Associates, Inc.; 133 (TL) ©Michael & Patricia Fogden/Corbis, (CL) ©John Gerlach/ Visuals Unlimited, (C) ©Tim Wright/Corbis, (C) ©William J. Weber/Visuals Unlimited, (CR) Getty Images, (CR) ©Michael Sewell/Peter Arnold, Inc., (CL) ©DK Images; 134 (TR, CL, C) ©Michael & Patricia Fogden/Corbis, (CR) ©Rick and Nora Bowers/Visuals Unlimited, (CR) ©Kevin Schafer/NHPA Limited, (TC) ©Hal Horwitz/Corbis, (BR) ©Jonathan Blair/ Corbis; 135 (TR) ©David Aubrey/Corbis, (CR) Getty Images; 136 (BL) ©Kate Bennett Mendz/Animals Animals/Earth Scenes, (T, TC, C, R) Jerry Young/©DK Images, (TL, CR, CL, BR) ©DK Images; 138 (TL) ©Pat O'Hara/Corbis, (CL) ©W. Perry Conway/Corbis, (CL) ©David Fritts/Stone/Getty Images, (CL) ©Stephen Dalton/NHPA Limited, (BL) ©Michael & Patricia Fogden/Corbis; 140 ©Ian Beames/Ecoscene/ Corbis; 142 ©John Watkins/Frank Lane Picture Agency/ Corbis; 144 (Bkgd) ©Gerry Ellis/Minden Pictures, (TC) ©Breck P. Kent/Animals Animals/Earth Scenes, (BC) Corbis.

Unit B: Divider: ©Hiroyuki Matsumoto/Getty Images; **Chapter 6:** 145 (C) ©Steve Raymer/NGS Image Collection, (BR) ©Paul Chesley/NGS Image Collection; 146 (TL, BL) ©Barry L. Runk/Grant Heilman Photography, (BR) ©Garry D. McMichael/Photo Researchers, Inc., (CR) ©Richard Price/Getty Images, (CL) ©DK Images; 147 ©DK Images; 149 (Bkgd) ©Richard Price/Getty Images, (C) NASA; 150 ©Richard Price/Getty Images; 151 ©Thomas Kitchin/Tom Stack & Associates, Inc.; 152 (TR) Silver Burdett Ginn, (BR) ©J. Jangoux/Photo Researchers, Inc., (TL) ©Calvin Larsen/Photo Researchers, Inc., (C) ©Craig Aurness/Corbis; 153 ©Steve Dunwell/Getty Images; 154 (TL, B) ©DK Images; 155 (TL) ©Galen Rowell/Corbis, (TR) ©W. Perry Conway/Corbis, (B) ©J. Eastcott Film/NGS Image Collection; 156 (BL) ©J. P. Ferrero/Jacana/Photo Researchers, Inc., (BR) Getty Images, (C, CR) ©Barry L. Runk/Grant Heilman Photography, (TL, TC) ©DK Images; 157 ©Steve Shott/DK Images; 158 ©DK Images; 159 (TR) ©Barry L. Runk/Grant Heilman Photography, (TL) ©Michael Marten/Photo Researchers, Inc., (BL) ©Garry D. McMichael/ Photo Researchers, Inc., (BR) ©Jeffrey Greenberg/Photo Researchers, Inc.; 160 (TL) Brand X Pictures, (BC) ©Jim Erickson/Corbis; 161 (B) ©Philip James Corwin/Corbis, (T)